C000263772

MORE
OFF-BEAT CYCLING
IN THE
PEAK DISTRICT

CLIVE SMITH

Copyright ©, C.V. Smith, 1993

All Rights Reserved. No part of this publication may be reproduced, stored in a retrieval system, or transmitted in any form or by any means – electronic, mechanical, photocopying, recording, or otherwise – without prior written permission from the publisher.

Published by Sigma Leisure – an imprint of
Sigma Press, 1 South Oak Lane, Wilmslow, Cheshire SK9 6AR, England.

British Library Cataloguing in Publication Data
A CIP record for this book is available from the British Library.

ISBN: 1-85058-330-7

Typesetting and Design by: Sigma Press, Wilmslow, Cheshire.

Maps by: Clive Smith

Text photographs: Clive Smith

Cover: Orbit Design

Printed and Bound by
Manchester Free Press, Unit E3, Longford Trading Estate, Thomas Street, Stretford, Manchester M32 0JT. Telephone 061 864 4540

General Disclaimer

Whilst every effort has been made to ensure that the information given in this book is correct, neither the publisher nor the author accept any responsibility for any inaccuracy.

Preface

This book is a companion volume to "Off-Beat Cycling and Mountain Biking in the Peak District" and these two books now provide a comprehensive set of routes with the possibility of many variations between them. This new book contains a collection of cycle rides which are suitable for the family as well as the individual rider. Some routes are easy whilst others are more arduous and they vary between 13 kms (8 miles) and 49 kms (30.5 miles), with some capable of being linked to give longer journeys. For convenience, car parks, railway stations and cycle hire centres are used as focal points, and there are generally Youth Hostels in the vicinity for overnight stays.

The routes lie both within and outside the boundary of the Peak District National Park, but are mainly in the northern sector of the Peak District. Sketch maps are provided for all routes but it is suggested that these are backed up with the Ordnance Survey 1:25000 Leisure Series – 'The White Peak' and 'The Dark Peak' plus the one inch to the mile Tourist Map. The routes have all been checked out on the ground for the condition of their surface and status, and the use of a tarmac surface has been minimised wherever possible; if tarmac roads are used, in general they have low traffic usage. Some of the routes pass over very exposed terrain so, if the weather is inclement, consider the state of yourself and/or your party before attempting a given route,

The description of the routes is supplemented where possible with notes as well as comments and photographs of points of interest. Inns and pubs are mentioned which provide hospitality and good food, but remember that it is an offence to be in charge of a bicycle whilst under the influence of alcohol.

There is a bright future ahead for cyclists in the Peak District. There is the possibility of a section of the Trans-Pennine Trail between Dunford Bridge and Penistone being opened during 1994; this could be useful for some of the routes which pass through this area and it may also open up further possibilities. Also, there is the possibility of a Pennine Bridleway being created, but this is not likely to be until at least 1996. This would be immensely helpful in providing suitable off-road routes through the Glossop area. Other authorities are also working on similar lines and the cyclist may well find additional routes being created.

In the meantime, I hope you get as much enjoyment from the routes in this book as I did in formulating them.

I would like to thank the many people that have given me assistance in compiling this book. This must include the assistance from the Peak District National Park Ranger Service for advice on some of the tracks used and for access to maps. My wife Helen must also be thanked for carting me and my bicycle around in my van, dropping me off and picking me up at odd places.

Clive Smith

CONTENTS

Introduction

The Rides

Route Locator

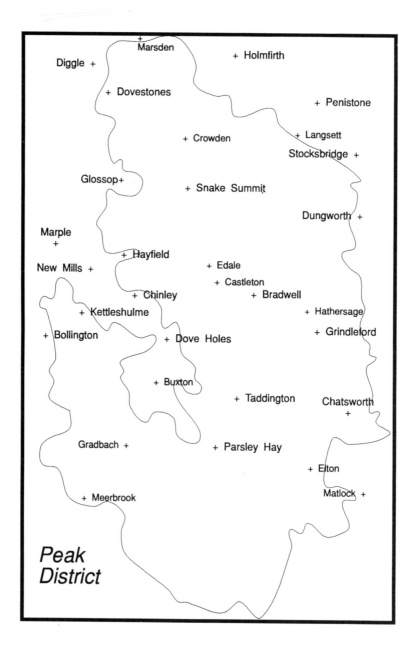

GETTING STARTED

Before you leap into the saddle and start enjoying the bike rides in this book, here are a few words of advice that will not only give you more pleasure, but will help to make you welcome in the countryside on two wheels:

The Country Code

When visiting the countryside, visitors are asked to follow some simple guidelines. They are mostly common sense and will help preserve the areas we like and love.

❑ Enjoy the countryside and respect its life and work

❑ Guard against all risks of fire

❑ Fasten all gates

❑ Keep your dogs under close control

❑ Keep to rights of way across farmland

❑ Use gates and stiles to cross fences, hedges and walls

❑ Leave livestock, crops and machinery alone

❑ Take your litter home

❑ Help to keep all water clean

❑ Protect wildlife, plants and trees

❑ Take special care on country roads

❑ Make no unnecessary noise

The Mountain Bike Code of Conduct

This code of conduct applies to cyclists everywhere but some points are particularly relevant to those visiting country areas and leaving normal tarmac surfaces.

Rights of Way

Bridleways – open to cyclists unless forbidden by a bye-law. Give way to walkers and horseriders.

By-ways – usually unsurfaced tracks open to cyclists. As well as walkers and horseriders, you may meet occasional vehicles which also have right of access.

Public Footpaths – no right to cycle exists.

Other Access

There are other places where cyclists may wish to go and these include:

Open land – on most upland, moorland and farmland cyclist normally have no right of access without the express permission of the landowner.

Tow-paths – a British Waterways cycling permit is normally required for cyclists wishing to use canal Tow-paths.

Pavements – cycling is not permitted on pavements.

Designated Routes – look out for designated cycle paths or bicycle routes which may be found in urban areas, on Forestry Commission land, on disused railway lines and other open spaces.

General Information

❏ Cyclists must follow the Highway Code.

❏ Use routes which you are entitled to use.

General Safety

❏ Ensure that your bike is safe to ride and be prepared for all emergencies.

❏ You are required by law to display working lights after dark.

❏ Always carry some form of identification.

❏ Always tell someone where you are going.

❑ Learn to apply the basic principles of first aid.

❑ Reflective materials on your clothes can save your life.

❑ For safety on mountains, refer to the British Mountaineering publication "Safety on Mountains".

❑ Ride under control downhill since this is when serious accidents often occur.

❑ If you intend to ride fast off-road, it is advisable to wear a helmet.

❑ Take particular care on unstable or wet surfaces.

❑ Use a detailed map for adventurous trips in wild areas.

Safety in Wild Country

The following recommendations are for your safety and are based on principles learnt through experience. Certain of these are just as appropriate to groups as to individuals. Although many people think of wild country as in the mountains, remember that remote and sparsely populated country areas can provide similar conditions, especially if they lie high above sea level. It's your life, you only have one, look after it!

❑ Carry spare food and clothing.

❑ Carry a torch.

❑ Carry map and compass.

❑ Carry a whistle.

❑ Carry a small first aid kit.

❑ Carry some spares.

❑ Carry a bivouac bag or tent to provide shelter in case you are lost or injured.

❑ Undertake journeys which are within your capability or the weakest member of the party.

Competitions

Events are organised by several clubs and national bodies. They can only take place with the permission of the landowner and/or highway authorities as appropriate. And finally – enjoy yourselves but remember others are also there to enjoy themselves – do not spoil it for them. Stupid actions by a few can cause serious restrictions for the majority.

Bike Types

While some indication may be given of the surface/terrain to be encountered on a route, it is up to the cyclist to use the appropriate type of bike for a given route.

Normal Bikes

These are generally designed for road use. The gearing is chosen for this purpose and the wheels and tyres are of a less robust nature than mountain bikes. Some bicycles are fitted with wider wheels and may be suitable for some less arduous off-road routes. If the terrain appears too rough, then the cyclist should push the bicycle for the rough stretches of the route.

Mountain Bikes

These bicycles are designed for the arduous terrain they use. The wheels and tyres are of robust construction to cope with the surfaces encountered in off-road travel. The gears provided enable the rider to cope with the steep hills encountered.

The Maps

The maps associated with each route are to give a general idea of the layout of the area the ride is in. The maps show the position of villages and towns. Road numbers and junctions are given so that it can be related to an Ordnance Survey map. North is always to the top of the map and a distance scale is given. The cycle routes are split into sections with 'a' always being the start point for the description.

The Ordnance Survey 1:25000 White Peak and Dark Peak maps are used for more detail. The following 1:50000 maps will also be useful:

❏ Sheet 109 Manchester

❏ Sheet 110 Sheffield and Huddersfield

❏ Touring Map and Guide 4, Peak District (1 inch = 1 mile)

The symbols used are:

| _____ | *Roads* |
| . . . . . | *Cycle Route* |

1. BOLLINGTON TO NEW MILLS

Distance: 18.5 km/11.5 miles

Route: Bollington – Middlewood Way – Marple – Roman Lakes – Strines – New Mills (golf course)

Surface types: Tarmac, hard-core, earth

Suggested start: Bollington

Map: OS Touring Map and Guide No 4, 1 inch to 1 mile

Notes: This route can be linked in with the Buxton to Bollington and New Mills to Buxton routes to provide a round trip. For an alternative route from Bollington to the New Mills area, see the Bollington to Strines Station route.

Refreshment: Various establishments at Bollington, various along Middlewood Trail (as signposted), Various at Marple, Fox Inn (Brook Bottom), Various in New Mills.

The Route

This route initially follows the Middlewood way almost to its finish in Marple. The route then goes through the shops in Marple, past the Locks and then down to the Roman Lakes. It then continues along the Goyt Way until almost to New Mills where a detour is made to miss the town, finishing near the Golf Course.

The Middlewood Way is formed on the bed of the old railway line linking Macclesfield, Bollington and Marple. The line opened in 1869 for railway traffic and closed in 1970. It was re-opened in 1985 for walkers, cyclists and horse-riders. The old railway has also provided a haven for wildlife; see what can be espied as you travel along.

There are various starting points in and around Bollington; the one chosen is almost next to the Groundwork Discovery Centre Cycle Hire place at Adelphi Mill. There are various leaflets about the Middlewood Way; unfortunately Cheshire only chose to produce a map as far as the county boundary – they appear to have forgotten the poor visitor who would like one for the *whole* of the trail from Macclesfield to Marple. It is requested that cyclists give way to pedestrians on the shared sections of the path.

The Journey

Section a-b

At the back of the car park go through the awkward gate where you do a 'wheelie' without being on the bike to get through. Turn right onto the trail and cycle down to the next awkward gate and then take care in crossing the road. Opposite there is a bit of open area with notice proclaiming Middlewood Way. Go through the gate with guide post stating Marple 12.2 km/7.6 miles. (Note the notice on the gate saying that this is a concessionary route and has not been designated as a right of way). This leads into the area where the old station used to be.

Cycle along, passing under a bridge, eventually reaching a gate leading onto a tarmac section, this is the viaduct over the central part of Bollington. There is a church on the right, followed by Bollington Arts Centre. The track now wends its way northwards with hilly country on the right (with canal) and the flatlands of the Cheshire Plain to the left. Along here, there are small wet areas with rushes, blackberries in abundance at the right time of year and a typical exhibition of how nature re-colonises. There are various routes marked off to left and right but remember cycles can only go on roads and bridleways.

After 6 km (3.8 miles) there is a Car Park at Poynton Coppice, a useful place if being met, with a public telephone box on the right just beyond. Continue northwards past another wetland area and into a picnic area on the site of the Old Higher Poynton Station. At the north end is an exit to a road and the Boars Head pub. Continue ahead, Marple signposted as 4.6 km (2.9 miles). In about 1.5 km, we cross the still-in-use Buxton to Manchester railway line (with station for the weary!). Just prior to this would have been a turn off to the right and a link to the Buxton line. Just to the north of this, near the power lines, is a picnic area, with a bar to tether a horse but no bike racks! Go through the gate and eventually finding a sign on the left which states Ladybrook Valley Middlewood Way, Norbury Hollow. Continue along the wider track, crossing under the A6 in a tunnel like structure and immediately into an area where the old High Lane Station was situated.

Continue, with varying views at about 10 o'clock of the urban sprawl of Stockport and Manchester. Past the entrance to Oakfield Farm on the right (cycle hire, eggs, hay etc), and off route picnic site on the left. Past a notice stating Rosehill – Middlewood – Macclesfield Linear Routeway and a chimney is seen ahead. On reaching the vicinity of the chimney, for New Mills turn right. To continue to

Rosehill, go across the large gravelled area and continue, eventually exiting next to a set of shanty buildings into a rough parking area and the car park of Rosehill Station further on and to the right.

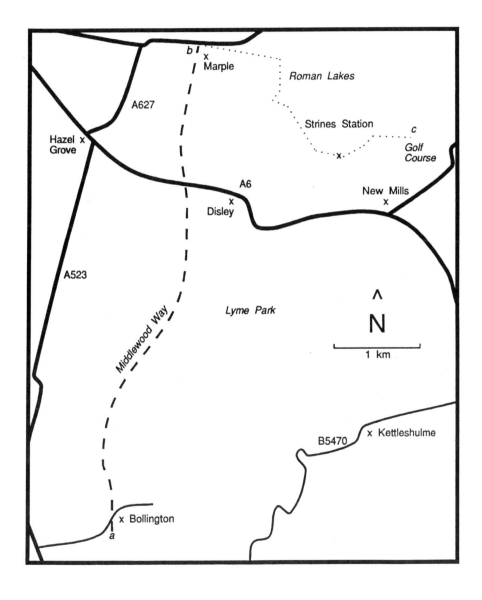

Section b-c

Having turned right just before the chimney, head into Wood Lane and continue to the staggered road junction. Here, go almost straight ahead into Buxton Lane, passing shops on the left. Continue up here, past Ridge College and to the T-junction. Turn left here and continue past another part of Ridge College and Marple United Reformed Church on the right and to the mini roundabout. Go straight across here and drop to the T-junction, here turn right as for New Mills and Glossop. Cycle up through a busy shopping area and over the canal bridge. Immediately beyond go ahead into Oldknow Road, do not follow the main road round to the right.

Drop down here to the next T-junction and then go straight ahead into Faywood Drive (No Through Road), signposted for Roman lakes. Drop down to the right, passing a nursing home on the left and then the railway (emerging from a tunnel) on the right. The tarmac surface deteriorates to hard-core, the track eventually swinging left at Bottoms Bridge and rising to a meeting of the ways. Here bear right as for Goyt Way (GW), Roman Lakes into Lakes Road – be careful with the traffic along here, especially on a hot summers day. At the next junction/signpost go right for GW and Roman Lakes and still labelled Lakes Road. The Roman Lakes are soon reached on the left where there is parking, refreshments, toilets, fishing and boating.

Continue straight ahead onto a narrow hard-core track with notice stating 'Bridleway, No Galloping' – a bit painful on a bike! Go down here, running parallel with the river Goyt – not looking very inviting because of industrial pollution. Pass under a large railway viaduct (carrying the Manchester to Sheffield Line), over a small weir and then a small cottage on the left. Continue past Roman Lodge, a guide post: the track then rises and drops down with a wall on the left and then parallel with the river. Follow the track round to the left as it dives under the railway again in almost a mini tunnel, the track swinging right as it emerges and then passing the farm at Windybottom.

Continue on the obvious track swinging marginally right, through what is often a muddy section. Continue along, past a retaining wall for the railway on the right, through a gate and then running parallel with the railway; signal NM101 is just before the next gate. Go through here and continue on the earth/grass track, drop through a muddy hollow and then up to another gate. Go through and turn right (as for GW), immediately before the farm building bear left onto the tarmac track and continue. Drop down here, over the railway bridge (Strines Station is to the left), eventually meeting a road.

Turn left onto the stone setts and rise up to the station information boards. Here bear left and pass under the bridge. Immediately turn right and start to climb on what has the occasional semblance of gritstone setts. This section is really a struggle for man, woman and bike. At times there is a brief respite from the climb. On the left is a deep wooded valley and away on the hill side is a part of New Mills. Continue always on the track ahead, through tunnels made from trees. A stiff climb exits at Brook Bottom opposite a white gate and a pub to the left called the Fox Inn – probably any kind of drink will do, providing it quenches the thirst. There is a telephone box here.

Turn right onto the narrow and walled tarmac road, rising to the brow, where you leave the Goyt Way. Turn left onto a rough stony track (with notice in the wall saying Clough Bank Farm) and rise up under the electricity lines, with golf course on the right – watch out for low flying white objects. The track eventually levels out as a farm track is met. Bear right and follow on the better surface until a tarmac road is encountered near the Club House.

The Roman Lakes

2. BOLLINGTON TO STRINES STATION

Distance: 22 km/14 miles

Route: Bollington – Oakenbank – Rainow – Back of the Crofts – Four Lane Ends – Jenkin Chapel – Pym Chair – Windgather Rocks – Kettleshulme – Lane Ends – Waterside – Hague Bar – Brook Bottom – Strines Station

Surface types: Tarmac, hard-core, earth

Suggested start: Middlewood Way car park, Bollington (SJ929712).

Map: White Peak Map (1:25000) and Touring Map and Guide 4 (Peak District, 1 inch to 1 mile).

Notes: This route cuts across from Bollington on the Middlewood Trail to Strines Station which is on the Bollington to New Mills route via Marple. It can therefore act as a short cut if doing a Buxton to Buxton round route. Minor roads are used quite a lot and the route is suitable for families, the roughest section being as the route drops at Lane End near Disley.

Refreshment: Various places in Bollington, Highwayman, Bulls Head (Kettleshulme), Fox Inn (Brook Bottom)

The Route

The route cuts across high ground from Bollington at the edge of the Cheshire Plain to Strines Station which lies in a valley through which the River Goyt and Peak Forest Canal flow. It is gritstone country all of the way. It passes Jenkin Chapel, climbing rocks at Windgather (if more exercise is needed) and skirts Lyme Park Country Park as it approaches the Disley area.

Jenkin Chapel (which has a secular appearance) was built in 1733 and the tower added in 1755. It is on the route of what used to be an important salt-way for the transport of salt by packhorse from Northwich to Yorkshire. An open air service is held here on the second Sunday in September.

The Journey

Section a-b

Turn left out of the Middlewood Way car park in Bollington and drop quickly to the bottom of Clough Bank. Here turn right on the main road, past Adelphi Mill and under the aqueduct carrying the Macclesfield Canal (controlled by traffic lights). Rise up the hill, passing a boat mooring basin. Cycle past St John's School on the left, over the brow and to where the present road turns sharply to the right. Here, go left onto a narrow road called Chancery Lane. Drop downhill, past the Red Lion car park and then swing left into Lord Street. This drops sharply through a works area before rising to a pub where you turn left, before going past a Baptist Church on the left and heading down to the road junction. TAKE CARE HERE. Turn sharp right (signposted Rainow) – NOT the main road – past The Turners Arms Hotel and The Cottage Tree. Continue along this road, past the Poacher, swing left and through the de-restriction signs, passing a Rainow sign as the road climbs. Follow the road as it swings right at the junction and immediately (just past a cottage on the right) turn into Oakenbank Lane with *No Through Road* sign.

Continue down this lane, which also forms the Peak District National Park Boundary, past houses and then – just after some cottages on the left – the good tarmac surface ends and the track changes to hard-core. This drops down, through a patch where the surface is wetter. Go over the bridge and then rising up to the right, passing through a section with holly bushes on either side. At the next junction, go straight ahead (i.e. NOT the track leading to the buildings), the surface now becomes more stony and rises to a summit. On the right there are views back to the Bollington area, the Cheshire Plain and White Nancy at the end of Kerridge Ridge. Now drop down hill on the walled track where eventually a tarmac surface is encountered at the outskirts of Rainow.

Turn left and rise steeply uphill through a tree lined section to Back-of-the-Crofts where you pass Croft Farm and Clarke House. Continue uphill on a now deteriorating tarmac surface, past holly bushes and eventually the summit – a welcome relief. The track now begins to drop and there are excellent views across the Cheshire Plain. The track drops past a cottage and stone buildings and to a T-junction. Turn right here and put your back to the Cheshire Plain, drop down and past Dale House Farm and a small Scots pine plantation until tarmac is again reached almost opposite Billinge Head Farm.

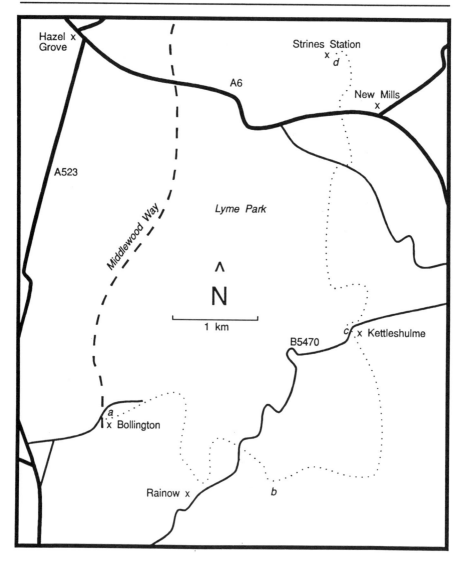

TAKE CARE HERE AS VEHICLES WHOOSH ALONG, turn right and climb for about 450m until the junction with the B5470 is reached at Four Lane Ends Farm (note for the thirsty: there is a pub just down on the left called the Highwayman). TAKING GREAT CARE, turn right and then almost immediately left as for Saltersford and Goyt Valley. Cycle over Pike Low (which is sometimes in cloud!) and drop down again, going round to the left at the road junction and past Old Blue

Boar Farm and then Blue Boar Farm. Just after this, take the track off on the left with a *No Vehicles* sign.

Section b-c

Follow this tarmac surface until it finishes at a junction with a track dropping to a farm on the left. Carry straight ahead on the hard-core surface, following the telephone line. As the track begins to dip down, at the junction bear right and drop downhill on, at times, quite a stony surface.

Continue down round hairpins and with a woodland on the right. Be careful dropping down as it can be quite slippery in wet conditions but take note of the idyllic scene below. By a barn on the right, the surface changes to gritstone setts and the gradient is quite steep – beware! Follow down until a tarmac surface is reached just before a pond. Bear sharp left at the pond, cross over Todd Brook and then rise steeply uphill, past the entrance to Hollowcowhey Farm. The road eventually levels out and just ahead is Jenkin Chapel (or St.John's Church, Saltersford).

On reaching the junction in front of the church, keep straight ahead for Goyt Valley and Kettleshulme. Pass the church and its graveyard and then steel yourself for the arduous climb ahead. There are plenty of banks either side of the road for a good rest and to sit and admire the scenery which is becoming more moorland in character. Keep going up until a road junction with Forestry Commission notice proclaiming the area as Pym Chair and a viewpoint. Turn left for Kettleshulme and Whaley Bridge.

Enjoy this next section as there are good views and the gradient is gradually downhill. Ahead is the gritstone escarpment of Windgather Rocks, a well-known climbing edge. Go past the rocks and then a cottage on the left and continue ahead heading for Kettleshulme. Ahead and to the left the B5470 can be seen, grinding up the hill. Go round the various twists and turns, eventually passing the 30mph signs and to the main road. BE CAREFUL HERE, there is a blind summit to the left.

Section c-d

Turn right as for Whaley Bridge and then left into Paddock Lane, opposite the Bulls Head pub. The road drops down through houses, then sharp right and past Kettleshulme Methodist Church and climbs to the next road junction. Turn left into Kishfield Lane, and then twist and turn for the next 350m, with views across to Chinley Churn. At the next unsignposted road junction, turn left onto the minor road.

Go through an arch of holly bushes and drop steeply to the bridge over Todd Brook in the bottom (this feeds Toddbrook Reservoir on the SW outskirts of Whaley Bridge). The only problem now is that all the height just lost has to be regained, so gird your loins and ever upwards. Pass the entrance to Bailey's Farm, over another summit and then another descent through a wooded area with stream on the left before rising to a road junction.

Turn right here, drop down over a bridge and then past Brownside Farm near the brow and then contour along, past Handleybarn Farm and the dismal looking complex on the right – Moorside Hotel and Restaurant. Continue along, through the road junction and begin the descent, away on the left is the folly at Lyme Park and below a reservoir. Eventually a road junction is reached at Lane Ends above Disley. The road notice opposite states Buxton Old Road, the road just used is called Mudhurst Lane. With a slight kink to the right, go across into Ward Lane and drop downhill on initially a broken tarmac/hard-core surface. Drop down past a white house and then continuing down and round to the left, passing a pond and white cottage on the left before meeting a junction of the ways. Here go ahead, dropping all the way onto a very stony track, the next few hundred metres provide a good bone rattling!

This stony track follows the stream on the left, eventually, after an eternity, the track crosses a stream flowing across the path and onto a more substantial surface, with a house on the right. Continue down to the main road at the bottom – the A6, so TAKE GREAT CARE. Go straight across and drop down past the Little Chef. Go under the Buxton to Manchester railway, past a transport depot on the left, over Peak Forest Canal and then under the Sheffield-Manchester line as the tarmac begins and drops down to the elbow on a hairpin bend. Taking care, continue ahead and drop down on the road; soon the River Goyt appears on the left and a bridge is crossed (with notice stating Waterside Road) taking the route from Cheshire into Derbyshire. Rise past two signs for Torside River Park, over another railway bridge and to a road junction, with notice opposite stating Hague Bar.

Go straight across past a cottage *(Toll Bar Cottage 1840)* into Haguefold Road. Continue the ascent, passing Lower Haguefold Farm, Haguefold Farm and Higher Haguefold Farm, after which the tarmac ceases and becomes a walled earth/hard-core track. Keep up the struggle for a tarmac road is soon reached where there is a seat for the weary just to the left. Turn left, as for Goyt Way, and drop into Brook Bottom with the Fox Inn. Continue down and round to the right in the small hamlet. Then turn left onto a track signed as a Bridleway. This rises steeply past Brook Bottom Methodist Church and notice stating 'Brook Bottom Conservation Area'. Continue up here on a mixture of surfaces, the track eventually levelling out past High Cliff before beginning to drop. At the junction of the ways keep to the track which drops (the rising track leads towards Mellor and will connect with the Marple to Chinley route in about 350m).

Follow down, dropping all of the way, with views ahead of high rise blocks. Pass through a farmyard and continue the downhill freewheeling onto a broken tarmac surface before approaching the railway line. Here turn right under the bridge at the junction and to the station notice boards – this is an unmanned station.

3. BUXTON TO BOLLINGTON

Distance: 21 km/13 miles

Route: Buxton – Burbage – Cat and Fiddle – Macclesfield Forest – Tegg's Nose Country Park – Kerridge End – Kerridge Hill – Kerridge -Bollington

Surface types: Tarmac and hard-core

Suggested start: Buxton, a convenient car park or arrive by train.

Map: White Peak, 1:25000

Notes: This route can form a round trip when combined with the Bollington to New Mills and New Mills to Buxton or the Bollington to Strines Station routes. There is a Youth Hostel in Buxton.

Refreshment: Cat and Fiddle, Stanley Arms, The Setter Dog Inn, Red Way Tavern and Bull's Head (Kerridge), various hostelries and refreshments in Bollington.

The Route

This route goes from the hills around Buxton in the Peak District to the edge of the Cheshire Plain at Bollington. It goes via Derbyshire Bridge, past the Cat and Fiddle, then via Macclesfield Forest and Tegg's Nose Country Park before reaching Bollington via Kerridge Edge.

Buxton is the highest market town in England. Although outside the National Park boundary it is intimately associated with it. The town dates from at least Roman times and even then was famous for its Spa.

It is worth taking time to inspect Macclesfield Forest Chapel. The present building dates from 1834 when it replaced an earlier chapel dating from 1673. Date stones recording both events can be seen over the porch doorway. The Chapel is built of pink sandstone which was quarried at Tegg's Nose. Each August the Chapel holds its annual rush-bearing ceremony when up to 600 people flock into the churchyard. This historic ceremony originally had a very practical purpose in providing a warm and dry floor covering for the church in winter.

Tegg's Nose Country Park is formed from an old quarry. Tegg's Nose Quarry produced millstone grit and closed in 1955. The country park opened in 1972 and is in two parts: the car park and information centre on the site of an old filled-in quarry and the main quarry site, which is about five minute's walk away where there are exhibits and good views all the way round.

On the last part of the journey to Bollington, you traverse the western slope of Kerridge Ridge, which is also littered with small gritstone quarries.

The Journey

Section a-b

From the centre of Buxton take the A53, signposted Leek and Macclesfield and follow this for almost 1.5 km, gradually climbing most of the way. Eventually a set of traffic lights is reached opposite a car showroom. Here go off at about 1 o'clock, with the showroom on the left, into Macclesfield Old Road. Follow straight along here, the surface eventually beginning to deteriorate. Cross the old railway line (part of the route from Cromford Wharf to Whaley Bridge, linking two canal systems), through a gate and begin the long ascent. As the brow is reached, the Cat and Fiddle can be seen on the skyline. As you start to drop, an old milestone is passed. Keep on the stony track until the Information/Ranger Briefing Centre is reached near Derbyshire Bridge. There are car parking facilities here.

At this juncture go straight ahead, rising uphill, moving ever closer to the Cat and Fiddle. Eventually the main road is reached (A537), unfortunately it is necessary to use this for about 500m. Turn right onto the main road, pass the Cat and Fiddle if you can without stopping, round the bend and start to drop.

As the road swings to the left, go straight ahead onto a hard-core surface near the chevrons and through a gateway. Continue here, over the brow and drop into the parking area at Shining Tor Restaurant. Go ahead to the main road again and cross over onto a minor road with a 7.5T prohibition order. The valley opens out, past Torgate Farm and down to the Stanley Arms on the right.

Section b-c

Turn left here and after about 200m take the right fork for Macclesfield Forest Chapel. Continue uphill and, just after the house on the left, take the stony track on the right with the *No Vehicles Except for Access* sign. Follow the track up the steep climb, in a slight hollow, running parallel with the telephone lines. After the steep climb the track begins to level and a house is ahead. Eventually a chapel with cross comes into view and is soon reached after coming onto a tarmac road. Go to

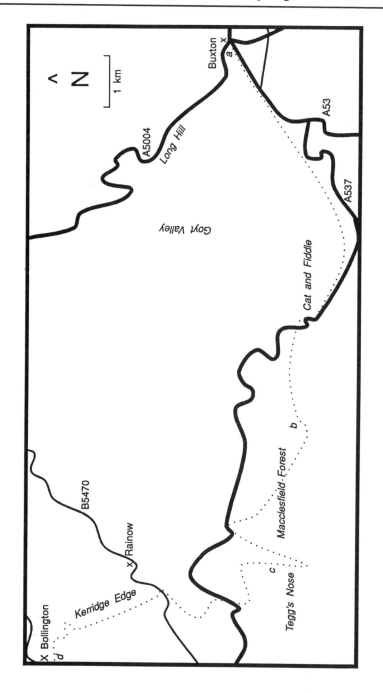

the left of the chapel and then right at the road junction onto the track with *No Through Road* sign, immediately before the house.

Macclesfield Forest Chapel

Climb on the stony track called Charity Lane, past a footpath sign on the left for Walker Barn, eventually reaching the brow near the microwave tower on the left. There are now good views to the right. Drop down the wall lined track to a tarmac road and bear right. Follow the road round to the left and then begin to descend. There are superb views ahead, a quarry to the left and the main road approaching on the right. Ensure the brakes are good here as the main road (A537) is soon reached opposite the Peak District National Park millstone symbol. On reaching the main road turn left. In just over 120m go left onto a narrow tarmac road just before a pub called The Setter Dog Inn. The entrance to this road has a *No Through Road* sign and a notice for Crooked Yard Farm.

Follow this road down, ahead is the microwave tower on Sutton Bank. On the near hillside on the right is a ruin and, just to the left of it, the visitor centre at Tegg's Nose where the route is heading. As the road swings slightly right and then left, there is an old Boundary Stone on the left with an M and date of 1822. Bear right at the entrance to Five Ashes and drop down, over the stream and rise again for about 150m, there is then a wooden seat and telegraph pole on the right.

Turn right here and double back onto a track known as Saddlers Way (an old packhorse route). Rise steeply on this paved and walled track, past a seat on the right and heading for the fence-line seen on the skyline. Just before a gate look on the left, there is a stone plaque shown in the photograph:

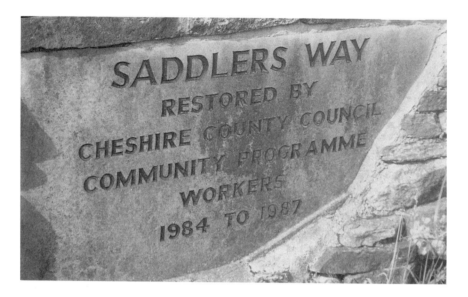

Go through the gate and on the paved track which then peters out into a rocky surface, finally exiting into the Car Park at Tegg's Nose Country Park. It is worth taking a look around here and visiting the other site some five minutes' walk away (unfortunately not accessible by bike).

Section c-d

Leave the car park over the cattle grid to the road, where you turn right. Cycle along for about 150m and then turn left onto a track just opposite Windyway House. Follow this track, swinging to the left and drop down, ahead is the large radio telescope at Jodrell Bank. Keep dropping down here, the surface becoming tarmac just before Eddisburygate Farm (a kennels and cattery). On reaching the junction at the bottom turn right. Cycle down here for about 450m when the main road is again encountered. BE CAREFUL as the traffic comes down from the right FAST.

Cross straight over here into the narrow road with 7.5T Prohibition Order Except for Access sign. Cycle along here to the next T-junction and then go left, initially dropping before the rise to the next road junction where a right turn must be made onto a narrow road. Drop down here, with views to Saddle of Kerridge ahead, through the houses of Calrofold. On reaching the next main road, B5470, turn right (BE CAREFUL) and cycle along for some 150m and then turn left into Lidgett's Lane. This climbs steeply and almost immediately there is a sharp left-hand turn and the road continues up past a grit bin at the roadside. This section of the route follows the Cheshire Cycleway. Beware of traffic coming down here!

Eventually the summit is reached. The road drops slightly and there are views across the Cheshire Plain. All along Kerridge Edge here there are small gritstone quarries, some still in use. A junction is soon reached at the end of Lidgett's Lane, here turn right. This road now contours along the hillside, past Macclesfield Stone Quarries and a stone tower on the left. Also on the left are views down to Bollington and the large outline of Adelphi Mill. Soon the 30mph signs are reached and the road drops down and round a hairpin at the Red Way Tavern. Above right on the ridge end there is a white monument known as White Nancy.

Swing round into Windmill Lane and drop down on the tarmac to the road junction. Turn right (Bulls Head above on right), over the brow and then down, passing a telephone box on the left and a church on the right. At the end swing round to the left and drop down (on Grimshaw Lane), passing St John's school on the right, Bollington Wharf on the left and to the traffic lights at the aqueduct. Go under here, past Adelphi Mill (with Groundwork Discovery Centre Cycle Hire) on the left and then into Clough Bank on the left and the car park for the Middlewood Way – on the right.

4. BUXTON TO HATHERSAGE

Distance: 25 km/15.5 miles

Route: Buxton – Peak Dale – Smalldale – Hay Dale – Batham Gate – Bradwell – Shatton Moor – Bamford – Hathersage

Surface types: Tarmac, hard-core, earth

Suggested start: Buxton Youth Hostel or Railway Station

Map: White Peak and Dark 1:25000 or OS Touring Map and Guide 4, Peak District, 1 inch to 1 mile

Notes: This route can link in with the Matlock to Buxton route. It also links with the Rowsley to Edale route at Bradwell (with possible link to Bretton Youth Hostel just off route), the White Lodge to Combs Reservoir route at Hay Dale and the Houndkirk and Stanage route at Hathersage. From above Bradwell it is also possible to go to Castleton.

Refreshment: Buxton (various), Midland Hotel (Peak Dale), White Hart and Valley Lodge (Bradwell), Marquis of Granby (Bamford), Hathersage (various)

The Route

This route starts in the limestone area at Buxton with its attendant quarrying activities and finishes in the gritstone area of Hathersage. The change between limestone and gritstone occurs at Bradwell Edge. The route links the Youth Hostels at Buxton and Hathersage.

Buxton was associated with Roman Times and known as *Aquae Arnemetiae*. The Romans built a fort at Brough, near Bradwell, known as Navio. Legend suggests that this fort was used to control slaves working in local lead mines. Part of the route used is Batham Gate which is an old Roman Road, presumably going from Buxton to Brough.

At Bradwell it is possible to visit Bagshawe Cavern. This is part show cave and part for serious potholing. The cave is open to visitors by appointment, the telephone number can be obtained locally. Instructions to locate it are given in the text following.

Hathersage is home for many commuters from Sheffield. Around the village are Millstone and Stanage Edges which offer good climbing. Little John (of Robin Hood fame) is buried in the churchyard and Charlotte Bronte used the surrounding area as background for her novel Jane Eyre. The nearby North Lees Hall is Thornfield Hall in the novel.

The Journey

Section a-b

From the Railway Station: Turn left onto the inner ring road and drop down to the roundabout, here turn left onto Bridge Street and under the bridges onto Charles Street. At the crossroads, turn right into Lightwood Road and cycle up to the main road – the A6, turn left, TAKING GREAT CARE.

From the Youth Hostel: Turn right out of the gate and to the main road, TAKING GREAT CARE, turn right and then almost straightway left into Dukes Drive. Cycle along here, under a viaduct and then rising round a left-hand bend and dropping to a junction with the A6 near a roundabout opposite Safeways. Turn left and at the roundabout go straight across onto Bakewell Road, as for Town Centre and Stockport. Cycle along here with raised pavement on the left, through the 30 mph signs to the next roundabout. TAKING GREAT CARE, go right for Stockport and Manchester on the A6 (Fairfield Road) and rise up past the Ashwood Park Hotel, under the railway bridge and then the pedestrian lights/crossing.

Both routes now join, keep rising up, round various bends, and through another set of pedestrian lights into more open country with the Devonshire Arms across the grass on the left. About 50m past the de-restriction signs turn right and go onto the hard-core track that crosses the golf course. Looking away to the left is the TV mast on Brown Edge. Drop down through the hollow with a pond on the left and then go up over the summit, with views ahead to a quarry works. Cycle downhill, past a notice to golfers about the fourth tee, until the tarmac road is reached; here, bear left.

Cycle along the road, with remains of a golf course on the left, then a 'blasting' notice on the right, before passing under power lines and to a Give Way sign. Be careful here because of heavy quarry traffic, bear right as for Peak Dale and Wormhill. Cycle straight along the road as it passes through the Tarmac complex, and then rise, passing a turning for Cowlow on the right. Keep on the main road until there is a house on the right, turn left here onto the unsigned narrow tarmac road with *Road Narrows* sign. This road undulates and gently rises until a level section is attained at the summit. The road then drops down past a caravan site on

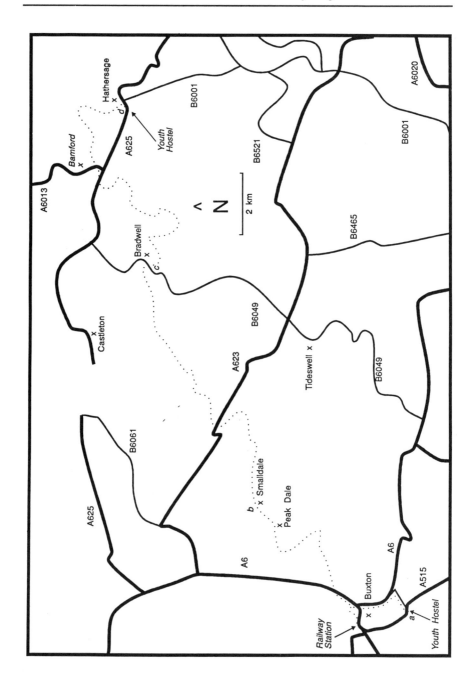

the left, through 40 mph signs and to a junction.

Turn right here onto the road with 7.5T Prohibition order. The road rises immediately over a brow and drops down through the village of Peak Dale. Go over the railway bridge just after the Peak Forest Freight Yard, pass the Midland Hotel on the left and then into the tiny village of Smalldale. The road swings to the right and, just as it swings back again, take the road to the right for Wheston and Wormhill.

Section b-c

Cycle up past the cottages and de-restriction sign and out into open country. The route climbs gradually on this walled single track road, over the summit and then a gentle decline to a junction. Go straight across here onto the unsignposted hard-core track. Follow this down to the bottom where the track bears left and parallels an interesting rock face. To the right is Hay Dale and to the left, Dam Dale.

Follow the track along the bottom and then climb as it bears to the right. This section, although hard-core, can be quite greasy with mud etc after a wet period. The track goes round various bends until finally it levels out and becomes quite straight. Pass the barn on the right with old railway goods wagons and rise to the junction with a tarmac surface. Go left here and follow along until the road drops towards a white house (Mount Pleasant), with good views to the left, and a major road (A623). Be careful here as you cross. Go slightly right and then fork left, signposted for Bradwell Moor. Look right along the main road here and you will see poles used for snow conditions.

Follow along the minor road which crisscrosses a Roman Road called Batham Gate. Pass the farm of Wheston House on the left and then pull uphill for about 1 km, passing a turn to The Holmes on the right. Follow the tarmac road as it swings sharply left and then right; the road is quite narrow with passing places. At first it is almost level before it begins a general descent, dipping down through quarry workings at one point. Eventually a junction is reached – turn right here, signposted Little Hucklow. After just over 200m the road dips into a hollow at the entrance to Moss Rake. Here, either turn left onto a short hard-core track to cut a corner off or rise on the road to the road junction and then turn left for Bradwell.

The road now climbs up to a summit before beginning the descent into Bradwell on a 1 in 6 hill. Drop down past a quarry entrance and then a notice that states *Unsuitable for Heavy Quarry Vehicles.* Across Bradwell is Bradwell Edge, where the route is heading. Go down through the 30 mph signs to the road junction. (If a visit is arranged to Bagshawe Cavern go right here for about 150m). Otherwise go straight across into Hill Head and drop steeply through stone built cottages, then the White Hart on the left and Methodist Chapel on the right to a road junction with telephone box opposite. Turn right here onto Brookside (not the TV programme, thank goodness!) and follow along with stream and green railings on the left. Note the house on the left with arch for Bradwell Brook flowing beneath. Continue to the junction, with Valley Lodge on the left.

Section c-d

Go straight across the main road and bear up to the left and climb, swinging to the right where there is a bungalow with the road name on it -The Hills. Pass a post box in the wall on the left with VR on it and then going straight over at the junction and dropping into a hollow on Bessie Lane. Rise out of the hollow to a small grass patch at a junction of the ways and then bear right with footpath sign indicating Abney. Follow this tarmac lane as it climbs, bears left and then right near a small garage when the surface becomes earth/grass. Keep rising, continuing straight on where the track swings left into a house, and a bridle-gate is reached.

Go through the gate and then go ahead and right to a hawthorn bush, where the track will be found rising to the right soon meeting the fence-line. Follow with the fence on the right through the bushes. After a hard push, follow the path round to the left where a stone wall begins. Pass a bush on the right, with squeezer stile half hidden behind, and to where the track crosses the wall-line. Here bear left with the broken wall on the left. A vertical stone slab is passed on the left with small hole through it and then eventually a bridle-gate is reached. Go through, pass a small rock face on the right before the track reaches the top and doubles back on itself and along to another bridle-gate. Go through this and then straight to the field gate with track beyond.

Turn right onto the track and climb gently, through a gate and follow on the wide walled track, passing Overdale Nature Reserve on the left. This swings left and passes a tarmac road finishing on the right (which leads to Abney). Keep ahead on the hard-core/earth track, following a wall on the right, the track soon becoming rutted. As a fence-line/gate is approached ahead, swing left and rise up on an unfenced section over a piece of moorland before dropping down and reaching a walled track on the right with gateposts. Take this track and cycle along to the next gate.

Continue through the gate on what is known as Shatton Lane. Looking across to the left you can see the route to be taken. Climb past the remote TV mast and the track then begins to drop. Take time to admire the views. Continue, through the next gate, and then onto a tarmac surface. This now drops down quite steeply, round various bends, the TV mast being clearly seen against the skyline at one point. The lane soon becomes bush-lined for a while, before entering through the houses. At the junction bear right and follow this tarmac road through the houses. This then swings left over the River Noe and to a main road with 40 mph signs – the A625.

TAKING GREAT CARE, turn right and continue along the road, passing a cafe on the left before entering Bamford on Hope Road. Go over the narrow bridge and then, getting off the bike, push it across a grass verge onto a road that has been cut-off. (The Marquis of Granby pub is straight on here, it is then possible to turn left and to the railway bridge). Cycle up this road until it comes to a junction near a bus shelter. Turn left here, over the railway bridge and then turn right (as indicated for Bamford Station) and cycle up Saltergate Lane. Pass Sickleholme Golf Club, and rise with houses on the left until a junction is reached.

Here go right through the speed de-restriction signs onto a road with *Unsuitable for Motors* sign and called Hurstclough Lane. Where there is a Private sign bear right and drop down to the bottom, with bridge over Upper Hurst Brook. At this juncture the track surface deteriorates, but continue and rise uphill round the bends on a sunken track – quite a pull! The gradient begins to ease and then swings left where a bridle route goes off on the right, continue on the main track whose surface varies between hard-core and tarmac.

The track continues climbing – phew – a track eventually joining from the right with *Private Road, Farm Access Only* notice. Keep the struggle uphill going, passing another track coming in from the left and then a Holly/Beech hedge on the left. The road eventually begins to drop, round a right-hand bend, past two houses on the left. It then rises to a road junction where you discover that this is now called Gatehouse Lane. Turn right here and then begin a long descent, passing a seat on the left and then a Bridleway notice on the left. Follow the road round to the right (Coggers Lane) at the road junction (do not take Birley Lane).

Pass a notice for Thorpe Farm Bunkhouse and, as the road drops again, Hathersage can be seen down to the left. Follow down through the 30 mph signs into the built up area, round a sharp right-hand bend and thence to a road junction opposite the Jaggers Lane notice, with an Edward VII post box. Turn left and continue dropping until the main road is reached at the bottom – the A625 again. The Youth Hostel is to the right, just after a row of cottages.

5. CHINLEY CHURN

Distance: 18.5 km/11.5 miles

Route: Chinley Station – Bridgeholm Green – Beet Farm – South Head – Hayfield – Sett Valley Trail – Birch Vale – Chinley Churn – Dolly Lane -Buxworth – Whitehough – Chinley Station

Surface types: Tarmac, hard-core, earth

Suggested start: Chinley Station. Please note that there is limited parking near this station. If the route is to be reached by car, the start point can be the Sett Valley Trail car park at Hayfield.

Map: Dark Peak (1:25000)

Notes: Although reasonably well defined, the parts of the route below Kinder and over Chinley Churn are exposed to the elements of the weather and so it is wise to be prepared for bad conditions. This route could be mixed with some of the Marple to Chinley or Rowarth Round routes. At Hayfield it can be linked to routes for Edale and beyond.

Refreshment: Varied refreshments at Chinley, Crown and Mitre, varied refreshments at Hayfield, The Grouse (Birch Vale), Navigation Inn (Buxworth).

The Route

This is a round route based on Chinley Station which lies on the Sheffield to Manchester railway line. The route leads from an urban environment to below the Kinder plateau, along part of an old railway and then over the high ground of Chinley Churn.

Chinley Churn is a hill of rough pasture and heather rising to some 451m (1480ft) just to the north of Chinley. Chinley was once an important railway junction, its grandeur is no more.

The Sett Valley Trail is formed from the old Hayfield Railway Line which was built for the Great Central and Midland Joint Railway and opened in 1868 and linked with the Midland line at New Mills. The railway was closed in 1970 and purchased in 1973 from British Rail and turned into a recreational trail after reclamation work.

For comments about Buxworth see the New Mills to Buxton route.

The Journey

Section a-b

Exit from the station along the footway and on reaching the road go straight ahead down Station Road towards the older houses until the road junction is reached with Lower Lane, here turn left. Cycle along here for about 200m and the turn right into Green Lane, as for Whitehough and Chapel-en-le-Frith. Drop down here, over a small bridge, pass the Whitehough sign and a small chapel on the left and into Whitehough Head Lane. Rise again and the just past a bungalow on the left, turn left onto a hard-core track and to a gateway. Go through here and continue, passing a factory on the left, opposite which is a 15 mph notice. The track now narrows slightly. Pass a small reservoir on the left, eventually passing the sewage works and finally reaching a tarmac road just before a bridge under the by-pass.

Here turn left onto what is known as Charley Lane, pass the mill and bridge at Bridgeholm Green, rising again until the main road is reached – the A624 – take care! Turn left as for Hayfield/Chinley and cycle along for almost 200m, where a right turn must be made under the railway bridge as for Glossop. Immediately after the bridge on the right is the Crown and Mitre. Go right immediately after the pub and then at the junction behind it turn left. After a few cottages on the right, bear right and follow the narrow tarmac road. Exit through the speed de-restriction signs and into open country. Drop down over the brook and then rise again, passing some dwellings and then a farm, here continue ahead onto the road with dead end sign. Continue along here past Slack House Farm, the turning to Upper Fold and eventually Beet Farm on the left.

The tarmac surface now starts to deteriorate as the route progresses ahead. The track is walled and after a while grass is encountered growing in the centre of the road. The track now climbs steadily. Take time to look at the views behind – if the cloud's not down! Pass through two gates fairly close together. The surface of the track now deteriorates further and the fields on either side are changing from pastureland into rough pastures. Follow round the double bends and continue climbing on a grassier track with ruts. Go through the next gate and follow up between the two broken walls. Finally another gateway is reached but can be by-passed by going through the small gap on the right. Looking back at the stone on the right with a hole through it, you can just see the year 1896 carved in it with other markings below.

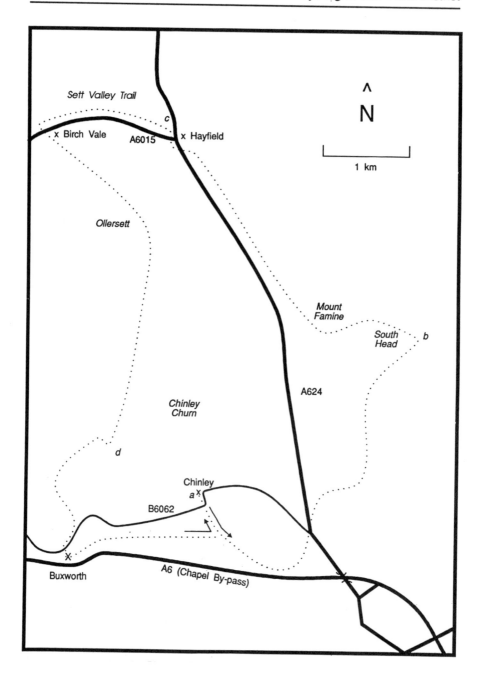

Section b-c

Turn left here and ascend the steep walled and rocky track up to the summit, admiring views away to the left. Go over the summit with South Head on the left, drop down initially on a stony track, past a footpath sign on the right. The track surface begins to improve but can be very mucky in wet weather. The track now contours along, with a steepish drop on the right into Dimpus Clough. Eventually an open gateway is reached, with a wetland area on the right just beyond. Continue until another gate is reached, after which there is a gentle rise. After the brow the track now begins a long descent towards Hayfield. The track is a bit rough in places, having been filled with old red house bricks. The track then swings left to a gateway with *Boundary of Open Country* notice. Pass through the gate and shortly after bear right on the walled track.

Keep dropping down. Just before a caravan and sheds on the right is a bridle way coming in. (This could be used to form a route via Jacob's Ladder to Edale). Keep on the main track dropping down before rising over a summit and thence into a sunken walled track. At the end of this bear round to the left and a tarmac road is reached opposite a stone barn. Turn right now onto what is known as Highgate Road and head down into Hayfield. Just before this road terminates at a STOP sign, there is a very steep downhill section – take care! Turn left and go down to the by-pass. Be careful here. Turn right onto the main road as for the Sett Valley Trail. Cycle downhill to the junction (about 40m) and bear left for the Trail. Pass the Kinder Lodge pub on the right and then, immediately after The Spinnery, turn right into Station Road and into the car park area.

Section c-d

Take the first road left and pass to the left of the Information Centre and head for the gate beyond – this leads onto the trail proper, do be careful of other visitors. Cycle along the trail, over a track guarded by a gate either side, pass a reservoir on the right and then a factory. The track soon swings sharply to the left and heads for a fence and gate. Go through the gate, labelled Birch Vale, and turn left and uphill to the main road and Give Way signs. Here, go straight across on to a rough tarmac road labelled Morland Road to the left of The Grouse public house. Cycle upwards, past the houses and continue for another 650m to where the present track swings sharp left. From here, go through the bridle gate and set course for Chinley, via Chinley Churn.

Ascend the well-worn track, following a wall on the left. The wall eventually veers left; do not follow this but keep ahead on the main track, climbing all of the time.

Eventually this comes out above Foxholes Clough and a bridle route joins from the left. Continue uphill and soon a wall joins from the right. Follow this up to the junction of the ways at a height of 426m (1398ft) with a three-way bridleway sign. Here follow the track round to the right, there then being a turn almost immediately to the left. Follow the walled track (or quagmire in wet weather), through a gateway and then follow a broken wall on the right.

Continue straight ahead where another bridle route comes in from the right, and to another gateway. Go through here onto what now becomes a walled track, to the left is Toddbrook Reservoir near Whaley Bridge. Follow this track as it slowly descends, somewhat muddy in places, until just after a small wind generator on the right, you pass through a metal gate and descend to a tarmac road beyond.

Section d-e

Here turn right under the electricity lines and follow round to another road junction, bear sharp left here and passing a weight limit notice. Drop down this steep road, ahead and below is Buxworth Basin where the route is now heading. Drop down past Laneside Farm on the right to the next road junction, here turn left and

Buxworth Basin

continue dropping on what is known as Dolly Lane. At the bottom where the main road is reached, turn right, pass under the double railway bridge. Very shortly Buxworth Primary School is reached on the left, just after this turn left onto a road with 7.5T prohibition order and head down towards the Navigation Inn.

Just after the last house turn left onto a tarmac road and follow round over a stone bridge. For those with a thirst to quench, turn left just after the Inn into the car park next to Buxworth Basin. Exit via the car park and join the tarmac road beyond. Follow this track, pass an old bridge structure on the left and then, as the houses on the right are passed, the tarmac ends and becomes hard-core. Follow this track along, under a 132kV power line and eventually coming across a factory on the right, after which there is a mill pond with ducks. Continue until the road is reached.

Go across here to the gateway and through the squeezer on the left. Continue along here until the next gateway is reached, just before a small building on the right. The point has now been reached where the route went off earlier. Turn left on to the road and follow until the junction with the major road. Here turn left, passing shops on the right and then shortly turning right into Station Road and thence the railway station.

6. DOVESTONES ROUND

Distance: 33 km/20.5 miles

Route: Dovestones – Mossley – Walkerwood Reservoir – Heyrod – Hartshead Pike – Lees – Roebuck Low – Delph – Diggle – Tunstead – Dovestones

Surface types: Tarmac, hard-core, earth

Suggested start: Dovestones car-park (SE013034). Alternative starts could be made from the car park at Walkerwood Reservoir (SD986991) or the car park west of Delph at SD967082.

Map: OS Touring Map and Guide 4, Peak District (1 inch to 1 mile).

Notes: On this route, most bridle-ways are indicated with a horseshoe. From recollection it also passes the greatest number of pubs! It touches on the Marsden route at Diggle.

Refreshment: Royal Oak (Mossley), Hare and Hounds (Luzley), The Junction Inn and The Peaks (Hazelhurst), Lord Nelson, Royal Oak and New Nook (Smallshaw), Red House, The Colliers (Hartshead Pike), Red Lion and Devonshire (Lees), Gardeners Arms and Bulls Head (Waterhead), Coach and Horses and Church Inn (Spring Hill), Roebuck Inn, Bulls Head, Swan, Rose and Crown and White Lion (Delph), Diggle Hotel, Cross Keys Inn.

The Route

This route shows how close the inhabitants of Oldham/Manchester are to moorland areas. The route goes from Dovestones Reservoir, a real day-tripper honey-pot, along moorland hillsides to Mossley. It then crosses various main roads, which inevitably follow valleys, up on to Hartshead Pike. It leads through built-up areas to the old reservoirs at Strine Dale. The route then leaves heavily populated areas over the hills to Delph and Diggle and then heads south again beneath the moors back to Dovestones.

Hartshead Pike probably formed a link in a chain of beacons stretching throughout England. There have been several towers on this site, the present one having been built in 1863 to commemorate the marriage of the Prince of Wales. Hartshead Pike is 282m (925ft) above sea level.

The Journey

Section a-b

From the car park, go down the side of the Ranger Centre, with *No Through Road* sign and heading directly away from the dam. Cycle along here, passing close along the front of some cottages, where the tarmac then ceases. Continue ahead on this walled track, rising all the way until a tarmac surface is reached near some houses and Oldham Way footpath signs. Continue ahead on the tarmac along the hillside, soon dropping down to the right and to a junction. Turn left here, on tarmac, signed for Kennels.

Climb here, past Hillside Cottage, parallelling power lines. Eventually, Noonsun Kennels are passed on the right and the tarmac then becomes dirt, continue along the hillside on the walled track. Keep on the main track, with Hartshead Pike on the hilltop on the right, until a definite junction is reached. Turn right here and drop back downhill, through a farm, from where the surface becomes tarmac, past a water treatment plant on the left before reaching a main road – B6175. Turn left here and cycle along for about 500m, passing Mossley Hollins High School, Abney United Reform Church and into a hollow. Here fork left onto a tarmac road which climbs above the main road, passing Micklehurst Cricket Club. Go through the houses and to a road junction, go straight ahead here, dropping downhill into Castle Lane and habitation. Follow round to the right with works on the left. At the end of the works, turn left onto a cobbled surface (DO NOT follow the main tarmac round to the right).

Go round the back of the works and head towards the hillside, just before this go right onto a walled lane with stone/broken tarmac surface which rises. Go past Winter Hill Farm and along the hillside to the summit. Now drop down, following power lines, pass through some houses and then drop right on the apology for a tarmac surface with runnel in the centre. Bear left in front of Lower Hydegreen Farm, then through Sun Green farm and to a junction of the ways. Go left here onto the fenced hard-core track (NOT RIGHT on the tarmac). Follow this track along until a tarmac surface is met at Walkerwood Reservoir.

Section b-c

Go right across the dam on the tarmac road and then swing left and cycle along initially in open countryside before entering a housing estate and Brushes Road. Go past a telephone box on the right before meeting the main Huddersfield Road

(B6175) opposite a telephone box. Turn right here (TAKING CARE) and rise gently uphill before dropping down the S-bend with the Royal Oak at the bottom. In the bottom turn left into Grove Road. The tarmac surface has a few pot-holes in it, so take care. The scene here is almost rural but with a feel of industrial desolation. Cross over a dismantled railway and then the Huddersfield Canal.

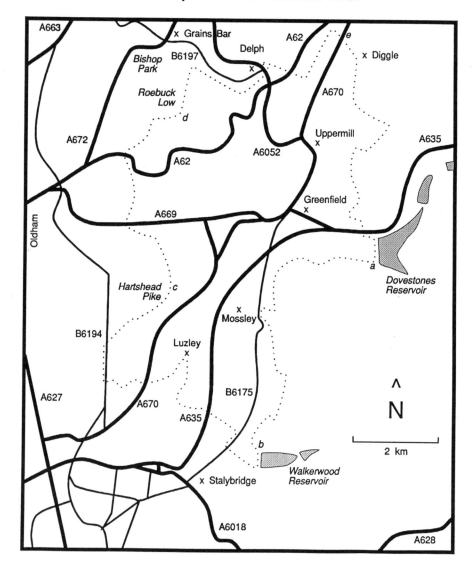

Soon an electricity sub-station is passed and an area reached of large green railings. Keep ahead at a junction, climbing uphill round to the right, over a railway and to the main road (the road just traversed is now called Spring Bank Lane). Go left onto the main A635 (TAKING GREAT CARE) past the Heyrod sign and then immediately right into John Street. The road turns left, and goes past a very small electricity sub-station before turning right and going steeply uphill. Follow the main tarmac track as it twists uphill, over a cobbled section before going back onto rough tarmac. Swing left round a building with *Beware of Dogs* notice and continue on the rough surface to a junction. Notice the multiplicity of overhead electricity lines in this area.

Go right at the junction onto what is known as Luzley Road and rise uphill on the cobbled surface, soon reaching tarmac near a white-painted house. The route is now on a ridge and there are views all around – some more pleasant than others! Soon a junction is reached opposite the Hare and Hounds. Turn left and drop down in front of the pub. Soon 40 mph signs are encountered near The Junction Inn, go straight across the A670 (TAKING CARE) into Gorsey Lane – with width restriction of 6' 6" – the barrier is certainly effective! Cycle on to the junction, here bear right – still on Gorsey lane. Just after a pub called The Peaks turn right at the junction -still Gorsey Lane.

Soon, with Abbeydale Close on the left, there is a road end and cobbles. Go ahead here on to a dirt track, along the backs of the houses and with fence and golf course on the right. Soon cobbles are again reached and an exit is made onto Gorsey Way. Keep ahead onto the tarmac, the road now drops and bears left, soon a pub is seen called the Lord Nelson; head for this, passing a school on the right. Continue past the pub and to the main road opposite the Royal Oak.

Turn right onto Lees Road – the B6194 – TAKING GREAT CARE. Cycle along this very straight road for almost 1 km, passing a pub on the left called New Nook. Pass the 40 mph signs, into a hollow and then, just opposite a pub called Red House, turn right into Lily Lane. Rise here, through the de-restriction sign and at a junction keep ahead onto the road with *No Through Road* sign. Continue rising up under power lines and back to green fields. The road now twists as it rises, passing a house on the right which looks as though it was a chapel. All the time the road surface is deteriorating. At the next junction, keep ahead uphill, with bridleway sign, and the walled track. This soon goes over a summit (with track to the left for the monument, before dropping down and swinging left. This then goes along, past a white painted house on the right, before meeting a junction of ways opposite The Colliers pub. It is worth a visit up to Hartshead Pike.

Section c-d

Just before the pub turn right (onto what is known as Back Lane) and follow along and then drop down to the right. At a junction, go right onto the walled track indicated with a Bridleway sign. Follow this track as it first twists and turns and then over the brow to drop straight ahead to a tarmac road, next to a house. Here turn left and follow Lane Head Road past the farm and to a junction. Turn left onto Knowls Lane and drop. This road then changes to Rhodes Hill and then Hartshead Street before rising to the main Oldham road – A669.

TAKE GREAT CARE. Go almost across to Benyon Street near the Red Lion pub, follow round and then head for another pub called the Devonshire. Almost in front of the Devonshire turn right and follow along John Street. Rise gently uphill through the houses, over an old railway bridge, past the Parish Church of St John the Baptist and the road now becomes Stamford Road.

The road soon rises towards a junction with a major road. Immediately before this, go right and rise to the main road. Go straight across into Hollins Road (which also says that it leads to five other roads). Continue uphill, exit from the houses and at a junction keep ahead on the narrow road that continues to climb. This road soon swings sharply right, with Higher Meadow Farm on the left. At this juncture go straight ahead onto the bridle route which is a walled track with grass surface. Follow this to a field gate, through and then follow the wall on the left to another gate, after which there is a wall on both sides. Down on the left is Strine Dale, where there used to be two reservoirs. This area is to be landscaped with bridle routes which could form an alternative to the present route. Continue past a barn on the right and to a tarmac road (Green Lane), turn right and head uphill to the Roebuck Inn.

Section d-e

At this complicated road junction, go ahead into the narrower road opposite, which rises and part way up is a *No Through Road* sign. Follow this, bearing left at the *No Through Road* sign on Two Acre Lane and continue uphill. (*Note:* if you go up the No Through Road, this eventually becomes a bridle route and rough track and continues through to a tarmac road; here, you would turn right – this route is not further described).

Rise past Highmoor Kennels onto the steep narrow walled road and a monument can be seen to the left. Go over the summit, with good views ahead of open countryside. Drop down to a road junction. The monument and a car park are along to the left.

Turn right and cycle along the narrow tarmac road which initially contours along the hillside before starting to drop, a bridle route comes in on the right which is the No Through Road route as mentioned previously. The road continues to drop, past a house on the left with many radio antennas. A junction is reached but keep dropping on Knott Hill Lane. The road drops down with a heather-clad bank on the left before dropping down into habitation. At the next junction, with lock-up garages on the left, go left and continue downhill to the next junction, in Delph. Here, TAKING CARE, bear left onto Mill Gate (opposite the Bulls Head). Drop down through the shops, passing the Swan and the Rose and Crown before crossing the river and coming to a complex junction near the White Lion.

TAKE CARE at this junction, go right, passing between a church on the left and toilets on the right, climbing gradually and the road undulates along, bearing right at one point into Rumbles Lane. Follow through the hollow and then up to the major road – A62 again. Go left and then immediately right onto a wide walled tarmac road that rises. The tarmac soon ceases; continue ahead uphill on the rough track, and keep rising to the summit where there is a house. Turn left and continue on a wide, walled dirt track which rises gradually. Hang gliders may often be seen along here, take time also to admire the views. Go over the summit and drop down round two bends (with Castleshaw Reservoirs way down below) before coming to a junction in a hollow. Take the track to the right by a wooden shed. Drop down here, swinging left round a sharp bend and down to the main road – A670.

Section e-a

TAKING CARE, turn right for about 50m before dropping down and back on the left (with yellow grit bin). Drop down and through the houses before rising again to a minor junction (this has been Carr Lane). Go straight across into Harrop Green Lane. Go through into the houses and sign stating Harrop Green, bear right of the green and then drop down to the next junction opposite a railway line. Turn sharp left here and then soon right over the railway bridge, signed for *Diggle Ranges*. Over the bridge a meeting of the ways is encountered, with Diggle Hotel on the left. Go right here as for Kiln Green.

Pass Kilngreen Church on the left and continue along, climbing up to a junction. Go left into Running Hill Lane. After about 250m, turn left onto a walled dirt/grass track and follow as it curves right and meets tarmac again, go left. (Alternatively you could go straight on to the junction and turn left). Rise up on the tarmac and follow right round the sharp bend. The road now drops gradually, with views down on the right of a church. Go down past the Cross Keys Inn. Soon after this a minor crossroads is reached, turn left just before the cemetery into Gellfield Lane. Keep on the main tarmac road (ignoring a fork to the right), above on the hillside is an Obelisk. The road eventually swings right and drops down to a road junction and Fur Lane.

Turn left here and then at the next junction, go ahead, rising uphill and then bear left. Continue climbing here, past a road sign stating Bunkers and over the summit. Just past the houses turn sharp right, then bear right again. Cycle along to the next junction and then take the left fork. This rises again slightly before dropping to the main road at the bottom (this has been Hollins Lane). Go left onto the main road (A635), TAKING GREAT CARE, and then shortly right as for Dovestones Reservoir into Bank Lane. Drop down over the cattle grid and curve right under the earth dam wall and then to the car-park on the left, just past the National Park Ranger Centre and toilets.

7. EDALE ROUND

Distance: 20.5 km/13 miles

Route: Edale – Hardenclough – Greenlands – Hollins Cross – Castleton – Old Moor – Brock Tor – Old Dam – Perry Dale – Rushup Hall – Chapel Gate – Barber Booth – Edale

Surface types: Tarmac, hard-core, earth

Suggested start: Edale Car Park or Railway Station

Map: Dark Peak and White Peak, 1:25000

Notes: There are Youth Hostels at Castleton and near Edale, camp-sites in both areas and Information Centres. The route can link with others at Edale, such as Low Bradfield to Hayfield, Edale to Langsett etc.

Refreshment: The Ramblers and Nags Head (Edale), various refreshment and hostelries in Castleton

The Route

The route leads from the gritstone area of the Edale Valley, over a ridge into a limestone area (and the honeypot of Castleton), through a shale area beneath Mam Tor (Route 1) and then back again on a different route. In Castleton there are various show caves that can be visited.

Route 1 (described on page 44), leads below the face of Mam Tor where nature has wreaked havoc with the road. The landslide occurred here some 3000 years ago and is recognised as one of the main land movement areas of the UK. However, it was decided in 1802 to build a road in this vicinity to miss the turnpike road up through the Winnat's Pass (a sign of things to come with proposed toll roads?). Since the construction of the road, major works have had to be undertaken in 1912, 1933, 1946, 1952 and 1966. The movements and havoc seem to correlate with periods of heavy rain. In February 1977 there was a major land movement, 600mm steps appeared in the carriageway and one side of the road dropped by 2.5m. The road was patched and kept open until 1979, with only a single carriageway by the major slip. In 1979 the road was closed to road traffic and has been abandoned.

The Journey

Section a-b

From the car park turn right out of the entrance, past the road into the village. From the station exit onto the tarmac road and turn right and down to the T-junction, turn right. For both routes, drop downhill for about 100m and turn in through the gate with National Trust sign for Hardenclough Farm and notice stating Bridleway, Castleton. Cycle along here, past Hardenclough Farm, picking up Hardenclough on the left. Drop down and over the bridge and continue up between the hedges until,

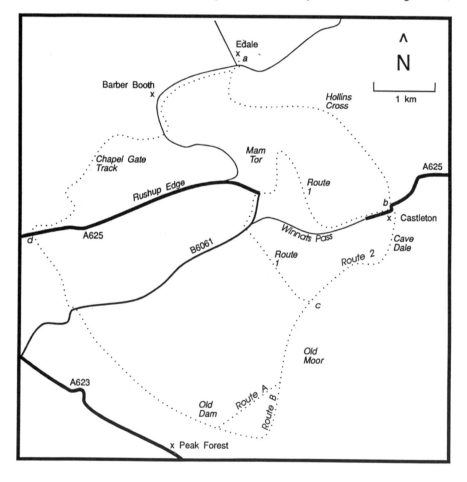

just before the house called Greenlands, there is a gate on the left at the roadside with guide post. Go through this gate and follow the route bearing left and signposted Hollins Cross and Castleton. Follow along the fenced (and initially hard-core) track to a bridle gate, noting views down the valley. Go through the gate and follow ahead on a grassy surface, passing between two small hillocks to the next bridle gate. Note the views ahead here to Back Tor and Lose Hill. Continue on the track, the gradient at first increasing and then easing, eventually meeting an eroded path coming in from the left, with footpath sign. Continue uphill until the viewpoint at Hollins Cross is attained, erected in memory to a Tom Hyett.

Here bear left and as the wall starts on the left, veer right onto a grassy area and run parallel and below the well-worn footpath which follows the wall line. After just over 100m pass through a bridle gate (and close) and continue initially on the wide grassy track for about 80m, then drop right (just before a *No Cyclists* notice on the route ahead). Descend past the gorse bushes, heading straight for the chimney of Hope cement works and to the next bridle gate. Go through and close.

The next part is not too easy to follow all of the way, so take note of the following instructions. Having passed through the bridle gate, continue in the same line with the cement works chimney ahead. Follow until the track just begins to level and then turn right into a depressed track downhill through the bracken. Follow this as it swings left and as it begins to straighten, here turn sharp right and head straight downhill to a bridle gate at the end of a tree-lined track. This route goes down about half-way between two electricity poles through the bracken and is just discernible on the ground. Take great care going down here. Drop down through a small hollow and on to the bridle gate.

Go through the bridle gate and continue down the initially rocky track, which also acts at times as a stream bed. Go down to the bridle gate at the end (where there is a wooden seat) and then out onto the tarmac and continue straight ahead. Pass through a gate and continue, round various bends to an apparent junction, here turn right (keeping to the tarmac surface) and to the next junction adjacent to Hollowford Training Centre. Bear right past the Playground sign, then Castleton Burial Ground on the left before passing over a bridge and then rising past a School sign to a road junction with the A625.

Section b-c

From Castleton there are two possible routes to reach Old Moor. Go straight across at the road junction passing the school on the left. At the next bend of the A625 the routes split.

Route 1

This route is longer but shows the ravages that nature can wreak on man's structures.

Follow the main road round to the right (Cross Street) and pass through the main part of Castleton which on a good summers day is heaving with visitors. Continue past the car park on the right and exit the village in the direction of Winnat's Pass. Where the road for the Winnat's goes off on the left, continue on what appears to be the main road with *Road Ahead Closed* notice. Continue along here, past a car park and sign indicating direction for Treak Cliff Cavern and *No Through Road in ³/₄ mile* sign. Eventually (after passing Treak Cliff Cavern entrance) a bus turning circle is reached with National Trust notice on the right stating Odin Mine. Keep straight ahead on the narrow track with a notice stating *Farm Access No Vehicles beyond this Point.*

Continue up here, when a notice will be found that tells the sorry tale of this road. Pass through the gateway and onto a wide section of road with signs of cracks and depressions in the surface and milepost on the left. Soon a section is reached where the right-hand side has collapsed. Continue on up, swinging left by the access to Mam Farm, and through the gate. Sections of the road are soon reached where total collapse has occurred. Here bear over to the right onto hard-core and find your own way through the maze. It is interesting to look at the broken carriageway and see how many layers of tarmac and hard-core there are, which shows the patching up that has gone on. Continue up, over another severely damaged section before reaching a bridle gate. Look up to the right and see the face of Mam Tor and possible hang gliders and parascenders.

Exit through the gate, bear right into the car park area and continue along the road until a junction is met. Here go straight ahead (as for Sparrowpit and Buxton, i.e. do not turn right). Follow up, with National Trust notice on the right for Windy Knoll, swing right with the main road where the minor road from the Winnat's Pass comes in on the left. Just after this bend (less than 100m), turn left through a gateway (white gate) onto a tarmac track with wall on the left. Follow this up, passing a line of trees on the left just before the turning to Rowtor Farm. Continue past this turning and onto the hard-core track and follow through to an iron gate with sign for Castleton via Cave Dale. Continue on the track defined by a wall on the left and a fence on the right. Continue to the next gateway and then turn left onto the new track and to the next gate. Pass through this gate and Route 2 rejoins here from the left. Turn right through a gate with notice stating 'Public Bridleway Peak Forest'.

Route 2

This route is shorter and goes up the spectacular Cave Dale but will require pushing the bicycle for the first part. Be warned, on a hot summer day this route will be as busy as a city shopping centre.

Go straight ahead into Back Street as the main road veers right. Cycle along here to the end near a small green and then bear left. A sign is encountered, pointing right for Cave Dale and the Limestone Way. Although this sign shows a pedestrian, this route is a bridleway. Follow this up between the houses on a tarmac path which soon ceases and through a mini gorge to a bridle gate. Pass through this and then prepare to push the bike for the next 1 km (0.6 mile). It is virtually impossible to ride as the uphill gradient is steep and the surface very rocky – in wet weather it is virtually a stream bed!

Continue the climb through spectacular scenery as the dale rises to the next bridle gate with Limestone Way notice. Pass through and continue the struggle, the track lying between a wall on the right and a broken wall on the left, pass along here and through a narrow gateway with two gateposts. The track becomes more grassy and looking back there are good views to the Mam Tor ridge, parts of Kinder and beyond. It is now possible to cycle but still uphill, keep following with a wall on the right to a bridle gate on the right. Follow the track through and to the next gate. Here go through and head for the wall ahead which comes in from the right. As the wall is approached bear left and follow the track uphill, passing two dilapidated railway wagons on the left and then to a gate. Go through and then almost straightway through another onto another track along which occasional quarry lorries travel – beware! This is where Route 1 rejoins from the right. Go straight across to a gate and take the route signed Public Bridleway Peak Forest.

Section c-d

Going in the direction of Peak Forest, follow the wall on the right, until a junction of walls occurs after about 650m, here follow the track as it bears left and thence to some gates. Note: at the time of writing there was a gate to the right but only a stile ahead although it is classified as a bridleway. There is now another choice of routes.

Route A

This is the easiest and suggested for the family party.

Go through the gate on the right and follow the obvious track with fence on one side and broken wall on the other. We are above Oxlow Rake and can survey the dereliction caused by past lead mining and now the reclaiming of materials that were then regarded as waste. The track begins to descend, pass through a gateway and then to another beyond. The track now begins to drop through a wooded area, the grassed humps being the remains of lead mining. At the end of the woodland a gateway is reached. Here, bear left (away from the farm) and head along the track for about 170m to the road and there turn left. Route B joins from the left.

Route B

This is a more arduous route and suited to the cyclist looking for a challenge!

Go through the gate ahead (at the time of writing there was only a stile). Follow up the field with a wall on the right, past a dew pond and then follow the wall round to the right, to a metal bridle gate. Go through and then follow with a wall on the right, gradually climbing but the ground proving difficult at times for riding. Plough on!

Go through the next metal gate with wire mesh and into a walled lane which begins a descent. Follow down here to another gate with Castelton/Peak Forest sign, pass through and then ahead to the fence and follow round to the signpost. Here go through the gate on the right and then immediately left onto the tarmac road and exit through the gateway of Cop Farm. Follow this road, passing several cottages, then dropping down and rising again from where a track comes in from the right and Route A rejoins.

Follow the road now for about 450m into the hamlet of Old Dam, exiting on the road called Old Dam Gate. Go almost straight across here, keeping to the right of the village green onto a single track road. Follow along here, over a cattle grid and onto the unwalled road through Perry Dale. This is a pleasant little valley. Continue along here, past a farm on the left and then exiting over a cattle grid onto the B6061. Be careful here, especially of the lorries racing back and forth to Eldon Hill Quarry just up the road. Turn left at this junction and drop down for just over 100m and then turn right into a narrow road at a road triangle with 7.5T prohibition order. Pass through the old gateway, past Whitelee Farm on the right, under the electricity wires and then start the climb. Pass a house on the left, then Rushup Hall on the right, a pair of white stiles, before reaching the A625 opposite a road sign. Note the tunnel vent on the moor beyond.

Section d-a

Turn right here, as for Castleton, and go along the A625 for about 100m and then take a track on the left through a gateway with bridleway sign. Rise up along here with a wall on the right on a rough surface to a gate, pass through and then in about 100m there is a footpath sign, bear left here. Follow the earth track, past an old wooden post on the left, round an S-bend and with views gradually opening up into the Edale Valley. A footpath notice is reached on the left (No.98, 1939) and proceed as for Edale. Away on the left is the tunnel vent for Cowburn Tunnel beneath.

The track now begins to descend but on a better surface, this route is known as Chapel Gate. Pass through the remains of a gateway and the track begins to drop much more steeply – be careful as some loose stones on the surface can make braking hazardous. The end of the journey can now be seen across the valley. Keep dropping until a wall is reached and then bear right and through the gate. Follow the track along now with a wall on the left, through another gate and continue. The track now becomes hard-core and tarmac and drops into a shallow defile. Continue until the gate is reached which leads onto a tarmac road.

Turn left here and go down to the bridge at the bottom at Barber Booth. Follow the main road round to the right and continue. Be careful along here as it is narrow and some motorists drive like lunatics! Continue along past the route where the journey started and back to Edale, the car park or the station.

Looking down Chapel Gate into the Vale of Edale

8. EDALE TO LANGSETT

Distance: 27 km/17 miles

Route: Edale – Clough Farm – Hope Cross – Hagg – Derwent Reservoir – Howden Reservoir – Cut Gate – Fullshaw – Langsett

Surface types: Tarmac, hard-core, rough mountain track

Suggested start: Edale Car Park or Station

Map: Dark Peak, 1:25000 and Touring Map and Guide, Peak District (1 inch to 1 mile).

Notes: This route does pass through some inhospitable territory. On a fine day the routes are obvious. If there is snow, the crossing from King's Tree to Langsett requires careful navigation and preparation for the arctic-like conditions that may prevail. DO NOT TAKE RISKS.

Refreshment: The Ramblers and Nags Head (Edale), Flouch Inn, Waggon and Horses (Langsett)

The Route

This route leads you from the tranquil scenes of the Vale of Edale over a ridge to the splendour of the Derwent Reservoirs and then over high moorland to Langsett. The ridge between the Vale of Edale rises to 367m (1205ft), the moorland between King's Tree and Langsett rises to some 522m (1713ft).

The dams of Derwent and Howden were built, in Gothic style, between 1901 and 1916 to provide a water supply for the industrial centres of Derby, Nottingham, Leicester and Sheffield.

Probably the most famous event in this area is the use of the reservoirs by 617 Squadron (the Dambusters) in 1943 for practice runs and testing of the twin lamps for finding the aircraft height above the water surface.

The tarmac road to the north and west of Derwent Dam has restricted access for public vehicles so they are relatively quiet but traffic can appear.

The Journey

Section a-b

From Edale Station go down to the tarmac road and turn right and to the T-junction, here turn left as for Hope. From the car park turn left out of the main entrance, both starting routes have now joined. There is now a journey of some 2.5km along the tarmac road, heading in the direction of Hope. From the car park drop down and over the bridge (Grindsbrook), past the houses on the right and then under the railway. Cycle along here, at first parallel with the railway, then to a group of houses and entrance to Edale Youth Hostel.

After the Youth Hostel sign, continue for another 500m and then turn left through a bridle gate onto a hedge-lined track with footpath/bridle road sign. Climb here, over the brow and then along to Clough Farm. Pass alongside the farm buildings to the end and the turn right, through the ford and the succeeding gate. Ascend on the track and through to the next gate with a Boundary of Open Country sign. Continue up the track across the hillside to the summit, where the track swings left and drops down on a stepped track, note the views ahead. Drop down now to the bottom and then swing back to the right for about 100m to a bridle gate on the left. Go through this and across the ford at Jaggers Clough and then go up the badly eroded track – please take care, especially of mountain bikers coming down at reckless speeds. The track levels off and then rises to a gate. Go through here and continue for another 100m to a guide post – the meeting of four tracks.

Go left here (signed Glossop via Snake) and on to the Old Roman Road which formed part of the route from Brough to Glossop (Navio to Melandra). Be careful along here as this is still a county road and you may meet four-wheel drive vehicles and motorcycles as well as mountain bikers, horse riders and walkers. Go along the sunken and rutted track to the gateway with Boundary of Open Country notice. Please note: there is NO right of access for cyclists off this track.

Continue along by the wall, rising over a summit in about 150m and then descend on a rutted section to the ford at Blackley Clough. Go through the gate and climbagain, initially following a wall on the right. Soon the final summit is reached where there are good views in most directions. The track now begins to drop, being quite steep at times with a loose rocky surface – take care! Eventually a tarmac track is reached coming from Upper Ashop Farm, opposite a wall. Turn right here and drop down, through a gate with Boundary of Open Country sign. Go over a leat before dropping to Rowlee Bridge and rising up past Low Barn (with chapel-like

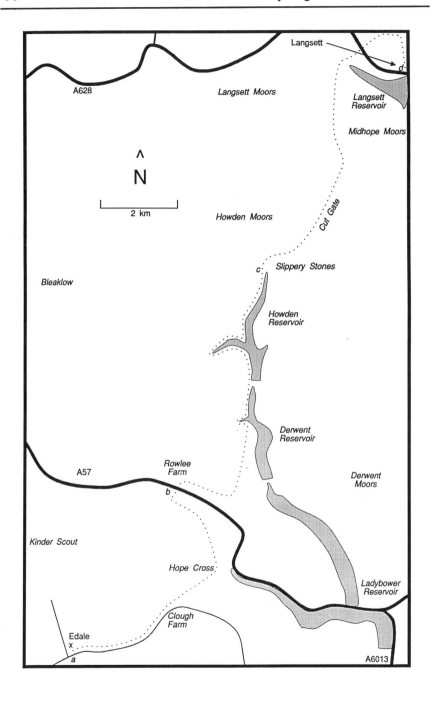

windows) to the main A57 where there is a No Through Road sign and bridleway notice.

Section b-c

Cross over the A57 and then continue up the tarmac track opposite to Rowlee Farm with National Trust notice. Continue up past the farm and to the left of a barn and to a gate with a *Lockerbrook 1 mile* notice . Go through here onto hard-core which soon changes back to tarmac, up through the two hairpin bends and thence to another gate. Continue through, still rising, the incline then eases before the brow and there is then a mainly downhill section to another gate next to a plantation. Go through and continue climbing from where the track soon bears left in front of a plantation and a four-way sign. Follow the track round (signed Lockerbrook and Derwent Reservoir) and cycle along here with a woodland on the right. Drop to a gate, go through, over the stream and then rise past Lockerbrook Outdoor Activity Centre on the right. Keep on up, looking to the right down into Ladybower Reservoir.

Go past a footpath sign and wooden shed on the right, and then climb to the summit (radio mast on left) and then begin the descent. Take time to look around at the scenery. Drop down, going through several gateways and then after a stream into the forest. After a while pass through a gateway into a less dense area and ahead is Howden Dam in all its glory. Keep dropping downhill, round various bends and then eventually a sharp right-hand bend and to the tarmac road, with sign pointing back up for Snake Pass and Edale. Turn left on the road.

It is now a case of following the tarmac surface for the next 5.5 km until the road ceases. Drop down and round over Ouzelden Clough, and then into a straighter section where there is a plaque to the drowned village of Birchinlee on the right. Keep along, passing Howden Dam on the right and then having to swing round a large arm of Howden Reservoir and over the River Westend. Climb slightly after this until the road swings to the left and there is a gradual descent to the end of the tarmac surface at King's Tree.

At the turning circle go through the bridle gate at the end and continue on a hard-core track. Rise initially and then drop down and cross a ford at Linch Clough. Go uphill through the trees and continue along, on the right you see the reservoir dwindle into a stream. At a junction keep straight on (do not go right) and in a few hundred metres the packhorse bridge at Slippery Stones is reached.

❏ *NOTE:* The 17th century pack horse bridge at Slippery Stones comes from the "drowned" village of Derwent. It was re-erected in 1959.

Section c-d

Another word of warning: this section of the route passes over inhospitable terrain, consider your state of fitness, the time of day, the weather conditions etc. This section will take a minimum of about 2 hours.

Go over the bridge and then bear to the left, passing a fenced enclosure, to two notices – one stating National Trust, Derwent Estate and the other a bridleway notice for Langsett and the Flouch Inn. This is the intended route and is known as the Cut Gate Track. Follow the track, through the ford and bearing right to another junction with National Trust sign for Howden Moor. Here bear right off the more major track and onto the one with a bridleway sign. Follow Cranberry Clough on the right, on a rougher and narrower track until a stream comes in from the left (Bull Clough). Cross over this stream and then go up, on a very rough track, the nose of the hill on the left (DO NOT follow either stream bed). This track rises steeply and is almost impossible to cycle up. The track then bears to the left and (BE CAREFUL) across the top of a small disused quarry – the track beginning to disintegrate!

Keep following the track, first round to the right onto a more grassy/peat base and then swinging uphill to the left and passing behind the small knoll. Have a good look around, the views are superb on a good day. Pass a couple of small cairns on the right before entering an area of boggy morass – I saw no remains of walkers or cyclists here! On a clear day you can see the track wending ahead and up to the skyline at a wooden post. Keep squelching on until the track rises after, what seems a long time, up to the post (mentioned above) in the middle of a cairn at Cut Gate End. After this, the main rise only continues for about another 200m before entering a flatter and small depression which is a scene of boggy desolation.

For the next few hundred metres, you spend most of the time trying to find the best route through, although there are odd scattered cairns. Eventually the route shows signs of descent – follow the route carefully, do not turn up any stream beds. The track rises at one point and far-off habitation can be seen. The track then drops marginally only to rise up after more wet bog to the small nick on the skyline. As this nick is traversed, and on a clear day, we can see dead ahead in the distance the concrete structure of the Emley Moor TV mast with white top.

The long descent begins, at one point joining a stream bed as you aim towards the head of a valley bearing to the left. As this valley is approached (Mickleden), the small stream is at first on the right before crossing and departing down to the left. The track now widens as it crosses the head of the valley. The path now narrows again and the track contours ahead, along Mickleden Edge. Although barely perceptible, the track now has a general downhill gradient. As this section is now traversed various views open up ahead, the Emley Moor mast is ahead and the Holme Moss mast is to the left. Eventually a footpath sign is reached and the parting of the ways.

Bear right and over the shoulder and signposted Langsett. This route leads down to Langsett Reservoir, from where you turn right for Upper Midhope – this route is not further described but can be clearly seen on the OS map.

The route described continues dropping here (straight on) and is signposted for Flouch Inn and Hazlehead. After just over 500m, you pass a Boundary of Open Country sign and broken wall. Drop down over a stream and then up and over Hingcliff Common and then down through several broken wall lines with Langsett Reservoir being seen for the first time on the right. After several walls, cross at an acute angle where there is a pair of gritstone gate posts. Pass over the wall and continue unabated downhill. NOTE: another bridle way leaves to the right here, running above the reservoir before joining up with the bridle way from the previous waymark and thence into Upper Midhope – this route is not described.

The route eventually reaches some trees on the right and a wall comes in from the left to form a throat. Follow this track down and round, eventually levelling out with a wall on the right. A Boundary of Open Country notice is then reached; go right and through the bridle gate with attendant sign and cross over the bridge (The Porter or Little Don River). The track then rises to the right and then swings left (follow the blue arrows which denote the bridleway, DO NOT take the routes signified by yellow arrows which are footpaths only). Follow the hard-core track through the trees and, after almost 300m, a junction is reached with signposts; bear to the right, rising slightly. Follow round the S-bend and then along the straight section up to the gates just before the busy A616. Turn left for the Flouch Inn (600m) on a busy road with attendant heavy lorry traffic.

Just opposite this exit, on the other side of the road is a picnic site and car-park with obvious entrances – a suitable meeting point. For Langsett turn right, take either the bridleway or the murderous A616 (which to be honest is easier going underwheel). Go along for about 300m and then take a signed walled track on the left (opposite side of road if on bridleway) which rises past a bungalow and farm buildings. Climb up this track, onto a level section and then follow round to the right and continue until a tarmac road is met. Turn right onto this road, over the brow and follow down round the bends to the main A616 again. Here, be careful and turn left as for Sheffield, after 100m or so turning right just before the Waggon and Horses into the hamlet of Langsett.

9. HOLME MOSS

Distance: 26.5 km/16.5 miles

Route: Holme Moss – Holme – Bradshaw – Meltham – Netherthong – Holmfirth – Arrunden – Ramsden – Yateholme Reservoir – Holme Moss

Surface types: Tarmac, hard-core, earth

Suggested start: Holme Moss car park (SE097038)

Map: OS Touring Map and Guide 4, Peak District (1 inch to 1 mile) and part of Dark Peak (1:25000)

Notes: This route can be linked to the Redmires to Holmbridge and Marsden routes. There is an Information Centre in Holmfirth.

Refreshment: Fleece Inn (Holme), Clothiers Arms (Netherthong), Royal Oak (Thongsbridge)

The Route

This is a route round the Holme Valley, better known as Summer Wine Country; there is no guarantee that Foggy, Compo, Clegg and Nora Batty will be seen. For those who want to see the houses and Sid's cafe it is worth a visit around Holmfirth.

The history of this area includes the growth of the textile industry with its use of water power and the surrounding hills for sheep. Weavers used to work from loom chambers in houses which have distinctive rows of mullioned windows. Many older buildings are built from Yorkshire sandstone and millstone grit and can be seen in places such as Netherthong, Upperthong and Holme which the route visits.

The route starts from near to the BBC Holme Moss TV mast, some 524m (1718ft) above sea level. It is a main transmitter for VHF radio programmes of the BBC. Away to the NE is the main mast of Emley Moor. Also on this route is a large white wind generator.

The Journey

Section a-b

Turn right out of the car-park opposite the Holme Moss antenna and drop down northwards. Follow down round the bends, admiring the views that are presented. Round the sharp hairpin (where the return route emerges from between the barriers) and continue down, exiting past the National Park Symbol, over the bridge where the road begins to level out and through the 30 mph sign. A cottage is passed on the right belonging to Huddersfield Girl Guides and the road then begins

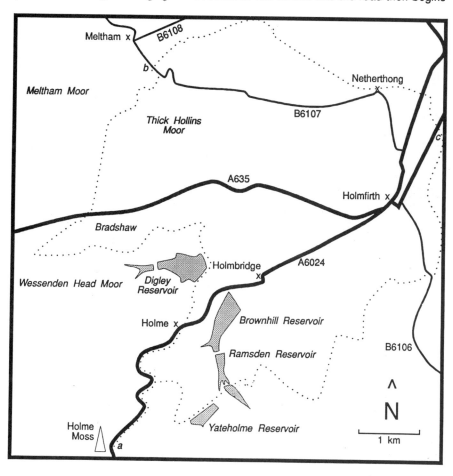

to drop and past the Holme sign. The Fleece Inn is passed and then, just after a '1 in 10 hill' sign, go left as for Digley Dam and car-park.

Drop down the road, eventually coming to a small car-park just before Digley Dam. Go over the dam, swing sharply round to the left and then rise past a picnic site. Keep climbing, past another car-park with picnic tables with a sign to Digley Reservoir and head to the crossroads. Turn left here for Greenfield. The road drops past a seat and as it bears right take the gated track that goes off ahead next to a house. There are Public Bridleway and No Motor Cycles notices on the gate.

Digley Reservoir

Cycle along this walled hard-core track, occasionally taking time to look about. Keep on the main track ahead, passing two stone barns on the left. Keep on the track heading always towards a house in the distance, This gradually gets closer and is then passed and some 500m past this a hairpin is encountered with stile and footpath sign for Wessenden Head Moor. Double back to the right here on the partially walled track that rises. Pulling up here, the main road above is soon seen and the track is paved with gritstone slabs. Keep going until a gate is reached at roadside with *Public Bridleway* notice – the height here is 399m (1309ft) above sea level.

TAKING CARE, go right onto what is the A635 for about 50m and then turn left at the Public Bridleway notice, through a metal gate and go past a boulder barricade to the summit and bridle gate beyond. It's as if you're on top of the world. Now begin the long descent to Meltham below. Ahead are views to Blackmoorfoot Reservoir, Slaithwaite and the outskirts of Huddersfield. A boggy section is reached after a while and then beyond, a gate which leads onto a walled track.

Follow the initial grassy surface, soon leading onto hard-core at a farm entrance. The track drops and, at one point a tower can be seen on a hill-top straight ahead. Houses are soon passed and the road becomes tarmac, not long after a junction is reached, go left. Keep dropping now down the various twists and turns and eventually a major road (B6107) is encountered on the outskirts of Meltham.

Section b-c

TAKING GREAT CARE, turn left, over the bridge and then as the road begins to rise turn right into Mill Bank Road. Cycle along here for about 500m and then enter a one-way section as the road drops down to a junction with pillar box in the wall opposite. Turn right and then shortly follow the road round to the left and uphill – time to push! Go past Meltham Mills Industrial Estate, past the de-restriction signs and finally to the summit – phew! The road begins to drop and passes a small woodland on the right. At the end of this (opposite Honley Livery Stables) turn right into Wood Nook Lane. Cycle along here, past Honey Head and the S-bends, keeping on the tarmac all of the way to a crossroads.

Go straight across here into Oldfield Road and then after about 300m, just past some houses turn right into Miry Lane. Being careful, drop down this very steep narrow road, go through the 30 mph signs keep on Miry Lane as it rises to the right (near Dean Brook Road). A chapel-like building is soon encountered on the left. Immediately past this, turn into Giles Street, passing Netherthong Post Office to the next junction. Turn left into School Street, passing the Clothiers Arms on the left. This road soon becomes Thong Lane, drop down the 1 in 6 hill and the walled section and then the bends and finally to a road junction at the bottom, A6024.

TAKING GREAT CARE, cross over into Miry Lane again (where has it been for the last kilometre?), this road is signed for Brockholes. Drop down here, past Thongsbridge Post Office and the Royal Oak. Go over the bridge (River Holme) and then begin to rise slightly. Just past the Parish Church of St Andrew, Thongsbridge, take a track off on the right called Berry Bank Lane and with Public Bridleway sign. Rise up here and soon a junction is met, go left and follow the fence-line along the back of the houses. This track passes through some bollards, then a short cobbled section, rising up between some sheds and then on to the main road above (A635) next to a Texaco garage.

Section c-a

TAKING CARE AGAIN, go straight across into Bank Lane and go to the next junction; here go left for about 20m and then sharp right into Cliff Road which continues uphill through the houses. As the road begins to drop go left into Meadow Bank, go past a seat and then just before the next lamp post on the right (before the bungalow) turn right onto a dirt track. This now contours along the hillside, with a road down below, there are views ahead to Holmfirth. At a junction keep ahead on the rising track, passing a seat on the left, at the next junction go marginally left into the walled track and head towards the electricity pole. The wall on the right soon becomes a fence and the track descends gradually. Ahead on the skyline is Holme Moss TV mast and, slightly left, a white wind generator. The track eventually veers right and drops down onto tarmac.

Go left and uphill round various S-bends to a junction with two parts, keep right at both. Cycle along to the next junction (the road just traversed is called Stake Lane Bank) and then bear left. Go into the houses and then turn right into Ryecroft Lane, follow this along through a few houses heading almost for the large white wind generator. At the next junction go right onto Cross Lane (ignoring the inviting track straight across) and then almost immediately swing left into Cross Gate Road. Follow this road down and round the bends to the B6106 at the bottom.

TAKING CARE, go straight across into Choppards Bank Road. At the next junction keep on the road to the right, dropping downhill, passing a seat on the left. Go to the bottom near Rowan Green Lane Mill, over a bridge and then around S-bends with gritstone setts in the centre of the road to a junction. Here go left, and just after a farm building abutting the road on the left, go ahead into a road with *No Through Road* sign and Lamma Wells Road board. Continue on this road past the houses and finally Arrunden Boarding Kennels and Tambora. The tarmac ends; continue ahead as the main track goes right onto a muddy grass/dirt track. Follow along and then swing up left before going right, passing an incongruous street lamp near the top. This track can be like a river or ice slide at various times!

Go uphill under the power lines (with box stating Arrunden A2523). The surface begins to improve as swings and a house are approached. Immediately past the house, go right and you soon reach another junction with a farm house ahead. Go left onto tarmac which quickly becomes hard-core, pass the entrance to Moorfield

Farm. Go over the brow and then drop down into the hollow before rising again, with plantation on the left, to a tarmac road.

Opposite, there is a Public Bridleway sign; take this – known as Ramsden Road. Follow this rough stony track, past Crossley's Plantation on the left. The lane bears right and the views are now down into 'Summer Wine' country. The track then does a sharp left and drops down on a stony surface to a junction in front of a plantation. Turn right and drop down through a gate. Follow the track round to the left into the woods, near a piece of rough ground (suitable for a picnic) and the map shows the existence of Tinker Well – beware of the odd pheasant!

Continue down the track and to a junction opposite a house. Go left and then follow round left again over the dam, take time to admire the views up and down the reservoirs here. Follow across, through the plantations on the main track, soon take the right-hand track (the more obvious) and continue on the dirt track. The track then swings right beneath the earth wall of Yateholme Reservoir. Pass over the reservoir overflow channel with Netherley Clough down in a steep sided valley on the right. The track soon goes round a sharp right-hand bend and goes along under the plantation. Follow along this gently dropping track, with views to reservoirs right and ahead.

The track eventually sweeps left and up to a gateway and cattle grid. Immediately after this take the track that goes off to the left and climb up to the road through a gap in the crash barriers. Here, TAKING GREAT CARE, turn left onto the A6024 and gird the loins for the final ascent back to the car park. Climb up and up and up, ever nearer the mast and the car park. Eventually this is reached and a well-earned rest is at hand.

10. HOUNDKIRK AND STANAGE

Distance: 27.5 km/17 miles

Route: Grindleford Station – Fox House – Houndkirk Road – Ringinglow – Redmires Reservoirs – Stanedge Pole – Dennis Knoll – Bamford – Hurst Clough – Hathersage – Leadmill – Leam – Grindleford – Grindleford Station

Surface types: Tarmac, hard-core, earth.

Suggested start: Grindleford Station.

Map: Pathfinder Series (1:25000) sheets SK28/38 and SK27/37 and Touring Map and Guide 4, Peak District (1 inch to 1 mile).

Notes: Although the moorland sections are well defined and should pose no navigational problem, they are exposed and can be unpleasant in bad weather. This route links with the Buxton to Hathersage, Redmires to Holmbridge and Rivelin Round routes. There is a Youth Hostel at Hathersage. The route could be terminated at Hathersage, where there is also a railway station.

Refreshment: Cafe at Grindleford Station, Fox House, Norfolk Arms (Ringinglow), Anglers Rest (Bamford), various cafes and public houses in Hathersage, Sir William (Grindleford).

The Route

This route lies completely within a gritstone area. It leads from the lower lying areas up on to the moors of Houndkirk/Burbage and Hallam. The route then comes off via Stanage Edge where many well-known climbers have learnt their trade. The track over Stanage, known as Long Causeway, formed part of an old pack-horse route from Sheffield to Bamford. However, the origin of the track probably goes back to Roman times.

The reservoirs at Redmires were some of the first to draw water from the high moors and supply water for Sheffield and date from the period 1836-54. The village of Hathersage has close connections with Charlotte Bronte's Jane Eyre and the grave of Robin Hood's friend, Little John.

The starting point of the route at Grindleford Station is at the mouth of Totley Tunnel which is some 5697m (6230yds) long. It was opened to goods traffic towards the end of 1893 and to passenger traffic the following year. It is the longest tunnel in the UK after the Severn Tunnel .

The Journey

Section a-b

From the station area follow the tarmac track uphill to the main road where there is a station sign and a post box set in the wall. Here turn left onto the major road, the B6521 – please take care. Pass the 40 mph signs with houses on the right and then through the speed de-restriction sign. Pass the NT sign on the left for Padley Gorge, then Yarncliffe Lodge on the right. It may be deceptive but it is quite a pull up here. Eventually there are good views to the left. The NT sign for Longshaw Lodge is then passed on the left and the country becomes more open, ahead and left are Carl Wark (nearer) and Higgar Tor. Continue to the main road, A625 signposted Castleton and Sheffield.

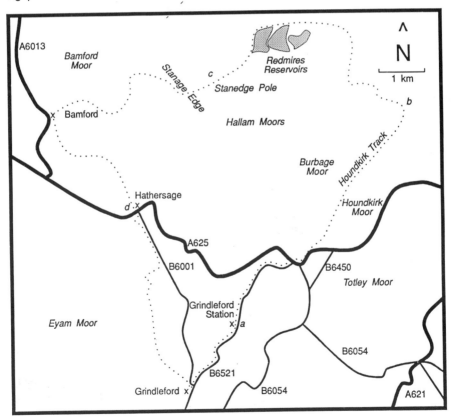

Here turn right onto the busy road, cycle up and swing left round Fox House Inn. About 400m past the inn, the main road bears slightly right. Here a stony track goes off dead ahead between some fences; take this track, known as Houndkirk Road. After about 250m a track is crossed and immediately a gate reached with Public By-way sign. Go through the gate and continue uphill on the track between broken walls, passing a green Boundary of Open Country sign and passing into more open territory. Eventually the summit is reached at 426m (1398ft) from where there are good views all around on a clear day! The track can be seen going off into the distance towards a conifer plantation.

Follow the track as it drops slightly onto a level section. Pass the footpath sign. Eventually rise up again, over another summit and then drop again on a rocky track, swinging slightly left to begin with and cross the bridge over Redcar Brook. If you look to the left, just before the bridge, you can just make out the remains of some enclosures. On the bridge itself, on a slightly larger smooth-faced stone, is a bench mark. Continue marginally uphill and dropping onto a sandy track, crossing another track and then levelling out, passing a stone on the left with RT chiselled into it, and on to the gateway near the edge of Lady Canning's Plantation.

Go through the gate, after which there are views of Sheffield to the left. Continue on this track, which then eventually drops onto rough tarmac before reaching a tarmac road known as Sheephill Road. Here turn left and head up towards the pub called the Norfolk Arms – be careful at the road junction.

Section b-c

Turn left in front of the pub and continue for only about 50m before turning right into Fulwood Lane. This road now forms the boundary of the National Park. Exit via the de-restriction signs. Go down and over the bridge at Clough Hollow (Porter Brook). Rise up, passing Greenhouse Lane and then passing to the left of the house called Buck Trap. There are good views away to the right of the metropolis of Sheffield. Continue along, passing Fulwood Head Farm and then Knoll Top Farm before a steep descent down Roper Hill (1 in 8) and to Brown Hills Lane, here go left.

Follow the road along, past a house on the right and then follow the road round a sharp right-hand bend and thence to a road junction opposite a house. Here turn left onto the road with dead end sign. Pass a small car park on the right, then Redmires Water Treatment Works on the left and eventually cycling along the railings on the left next to open water. Follow along, past a car park on the right, skirting round the reservoir, the tarmac road eventually beginning to deteriorate as

Roman Road near Stanedge Pole

the end is approached. At the end of the road (by the end of the reservoir) turn right onto a dirt track with Public By-way notice and follow uphill along the edge of a plantation.

The surface gets rockier and the going is a little harder. In one place the main track becomes sunken and rutted and it is easier to cycle on the higher tracks to either side. It is worth looking back and admiring the views of the three reservoirs which make up Redmires. About 100m before the gate, a paved section of track begins and on the right just in the trees is the remains of stone walls and a gatepost with bench mark. The track is probably an old Roman road, hence the odd sections of paving that are encountered. Go through the gate and follow the wall/fenceline on the right until Stanedge Pole is reached.

Section c-d

Go to the right of the pole and follow the obvious track along the fence, after 100m observing the short section of double paved track. Continue along, the track eventually bearing right. Here there is a wall coming in on the left. Look down this wall line and a gate post will be seen; this marks the route of a bridleway that drops down through Stanage Edge and Stanage Plantation, finishing on the road below near the unmanned Mountain Rescue Post. If this track down is followed, good map reading is essential! Otherwise keep on the present route which starts to drop, but which gets very rocky and at times makes cycling quite difficult. As you cycle along here, you are looking at High Neb.

Pass a Boundary of Open Country sign as the track begins to drop. The route is in front, swinging to the left to meet a tarmac road near a plantation known as Dennis Knoll. However, the present task is to negotiate this track to that point. Keeping dropping, past a rocky outcrop on the right, through a wall line with another Boundary of Open Country sign, the track the bearing to the left and dropping. The track surface very, very slowly improves and the going gets better, until eventually the metalled surface is reached on a corner with signpost for Ringinglow.

Go straight ahead here on the tarmac, through a gateway with cattle grid and keeping Dennis Knoll on the left. Drop down here to a road junction and turn right for Ladybower (if you want to cheat keep on the present road, the route rejoining this road in about 800m). Rise uphill and, at the summit, look back and admire the panoramic view of Stanage. Go over the summit and then drop steeply (with cement works ahead!), round an S-bend over Upper Hurst Brook and then a gradual rise to another summit. Here the road drops, past a footpath going off on the right and then to a small plantation on the left.

Immediately before this go left between the gateposts onto what is known as Bamford Clough or Leeside Road. Shortly cross another track, but keep downhill, over a concrete gully and steeply down hill. This can be quite slippery down here in wet weather, in autumn with wet leaves and in icy conditions – you have been warned. Pass two seats on the left (where you can stop to admire the views). Drop down with a small woodland on the right, eventually reaching a tarmac surface near a white gate and the entrance to Clough House. Continue downhill through the houses to a cross roads just before a School sign. Turn left here into what is known as Joan Lane. For the hungry and thirsty continue ahead for the Angler's Rest and a village shop, then retrace your steps.

Cycle along here, at what is an apparent junction, drop downhill to the right. This is a narrow lane, so be careful. Continue until a road junction is reached (almost a cross roads). Here go straight across through the speed de-restriction signs onto Hurstclough Lane with 'Unsuitable for Motors' sign. Where there is a Private sign bear right and drop down to the bottom, with bridge over Upper Hurst Brook. The track surface deteriorates, but continue uphill and around the bends on a sunken track – quite a pull! The gradient begins to ease and then swings left where a bridle route goes off on the right. Continue on the main track with a surface varying between hard-core and tarmac.

The track continues climbing – phew – a track eventually joining from the right with Private Road, Farm Access Only notice. Keep the struggle uphill going, passing another track coming in from the left and then a holly/beech hedge on the left. The road eventually begins to drop, round a right-hand bend, past two houses on the left and then rising to a road junction. This is now called Gatehouse Lane and has an Unsuitable for Motors sign. Turn right here and then begin a long, long descent, passing a seat on the left and then a Bridleway notice on the left. Follow the road round to the right (Coggers Lane) at the road junction (do not take Birley Lane).

Pass a notice for Thorpe Farm Bunkhouse and, as the road drops again, Hathersage is down to the left. Follow down through the 30 mph signs into the built up area, round a sharp right-hand bend and thence to a road junction opposite the Jaggers Lane notice. Here turn left and continue dropping until the main road is reached at the bottom – the A625 again.

Section d-a

Bear left here (taking care) for 50m and then turning right for Bakewell (B6001). When you have turned right, make another right fork just before the Little John public house and follow the railings and stream on the right. Follow this attractive little lane, under the railway arch, keeping to the tarmac surface all of the way. Pass under a metal railway bridge and back into civilisation. Up to the road junction and turn right onto the B6001 again and drop down under the stone railway bridge with adjacent 30 mph signs. Note the round building on the left – David Mellor Cutlery. Continue on this road, over the river bridge (River Derwent), the Plough Inn on the left-hand side.

As the road reaches a summit and swings right, take the narrow single track tarmac road on the right with a prohibition notice for vehicles over 7.5T. The road rises gently at first, past Hazelford Hall, and then after the next hairpin climbs sharply until after the next hairpin – height is gained rapidly in a short distance! Various dwellings are now passed on the left, most beginning with the name Leam. The road now rises and falls gently for the next 2 km, through wooded areas until, after a straight stretch, there is a left-hand bend and a rise to a T-junction. Turn left here.

Drop downhill on the 10% gradient, there are good views ahead to left and right. Go down through the 30 mph restriction and then to the road junction opposite the Sir William public house. Note: just before the junction on the right is a Pinfold which is worth looking at. Turn right at the junction and then drop downhill round a bend immediately to another junction. Turn left on the B6521 for Sheffield. Drop down to the narrow road bridge (over the River Derwent) with traffic lights. Continue over the bridge and then begin a long uphill drag for about 700m, just past the Maynard Arms Hotel on the right is the turning, on the left, which leads back to Grindleford Station and cafe.

11. LANGSETT ROUND

Distance: 29.5 km/18.5 miles

Route: Langsett – Fullshaw – Hill Side – Millhouse Green – Crow Edge – Broadstone Reservoir – Victoria – Snittlegate – Townhead – Dunford Bridge – Fiddlers Green – Langsett

Surface types: Tarmac, hard-core, earth

Suggested start: Picnic Site near Langsett (SE202011). Warning: it has a low barrier across at the entrance and is too low for vehicles such as Landrovers, mobile homes, caravans or even cars with bikes on the roof!

Map: Part of Dark Peak 1:25000 and Touring Map and Guide 4, Peak District, 1 inch to 1 mile.

Notes: There is a Youth Hostel at Langsett. The route links with the Redmires to Holmbridge, Woodhead Traverse and Edale to Langsett routes. It is close to the Stocksbridge Round and Holme Moss routes.

Refreshment: Blacksmith's Arms (Millhouse Green), Victoria Inn, Foxhouse, Stanhope Arms, Dog and Partridge (A628), Flouch Inn (just along road from picnic site).

The Route

The route passes through varying countryside – alternating between pastureland, rough pastureland and moorland. There are two sections which could pose navigational problems but there are ways round by road – take stock of your abilities. It can pose some hard riding for those that want it.

The route goes through some inhospitable territory, so prepare for hard conditions if bad weather is likely. PLEASE TAKE CARE along those sections of the A628 that are used. There is likely to be some re-alignment of the road in the Flouch area in 1994.

The Journey

Section a-b

From the picnic site/car park turn left, and take either the bridleway on the opposite side of the road (and running parallel to the road) or the murderous A616 (which is easier going underwheel!). Go along for about 300m and then take a signed walled track on the left (opposite side of road if on bridleway) which rises past a bungalow and farm buildings. Climb up this track (known as Brown's Edge Lane), onto a level section and then follow round to the right and continue until a tarmac road is met. Go left here and drop downhill, passing the houses to the road junction. Here go right onto the minor road signposted Hunshelf. This road now rises, drops, rises round a left-hand bend and then drops down into the dip in the hollow. About 100m or so after this, with the road climbing, there is a Public Bridleway notice pointing off on the left onto moorland; take this.

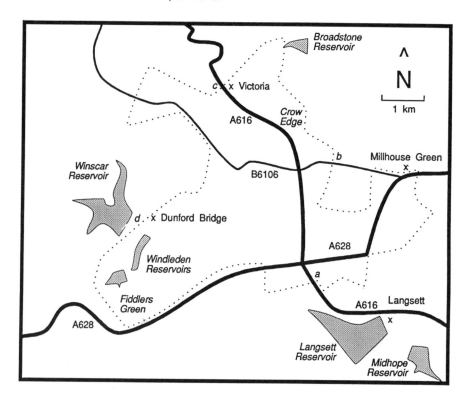

The track rises across the hill side (with abundance of gorse and heather), initially parallel to the wall below and a scattering of trees. The track eventually veers right and works its way to a bridle gate at the edge of the woodland. Please respect the notice on the gate – Please Shut Gate, Sheep in Field. Go through the gate and follow the wall on the right, initially dropping and then rising up through a broken wall from where the track begins to level. There are views away to the left here; cycle along to the next gate with wet patch just before it and a sign on it similar to that just mentioned. Go through the gate onto the walled track with grass/earth surface.

The track now has a gentle downhill gradient which finally begins to steepen as it drops down towards some houses, with views on the left down to the village of Millhouse. The track then becomes hard-core and as it swings left tarmac begins and drops to meet a road with Public Bridleway notice, opposite Bank House Farm. Turn left onto the single track road and then descend past various dwellings and cross over the old Woodhead railway line, soon to become the Trans-Pennine Trail. Continue onto Shore Hall Lane and keep dropping to a road junction. Turn right here into Birks Lane and continue, over the River Don, through the houses up to the main road (A628) with 40 mph and Give Way signs.

TAKING GREAT CARE, turn left onto the main road and into Millhouse Green and continue to the road junction, with some shops on the left. Here go right as for Holmfirth (B6106) in front of a pub called the Blacksmith's Arms. Continue along here, through the de-restriction signs, for about 600m to where, on the left, is a sign for BB Printing Ltd and a Public Bridleway notice. There is now a choice of routes.

Choice 1: Continue along the B6106 for another 1 km to a bus shelter and stop at the end of Hollin Lane.

Choice 2: Go left onto the bridleway (heading for the large white wind generator) and drop down to the printing works, go straight through the black metal gates towards the works and then slip round to the left and follow the stream to a bridge. Go left over the bridge and then turn sharp right and climb the muddy walled track and up to the white bridle-gate respecting the Private Grounds No Mud Please sign.

Go through the gate and then straight ahead on the tarmac to a junction. Here turn right, go through the gateway and bear left before turning right after the building, there being a fifteenth century chapel just on the right. Continue towards the buildings and then veer left to the gate posts and the hard-core track.

Continue down and to the left below a stone barn and thence to a metal gate. Go through this and continue on the walled track and at a junction bear right, dropping down towards the river on the paved section. Cross the stream in the bottom (track muddy) and then take the track going left towards the railway embankment and follow along until there is a bridge through. Go left under the railway, through a gate and then turn immediately right in front of an incongruous No Smoking or Naked Lights sign and electricity pylon.

Follow parallel with the railway before veering marginally left and to a gate just before a house. Go through this and continue ahead on the grass track with underlying hard-core. Follow this through to another gate, after which go immediately right and over the railway bridge (with another gate). Go down the walled track (with possible temporary fence across) and drop down towards the river. Go through the next gate and then to the bridge with steps. Go over the bridge (the River Don) and then cycle up the walled track which soon levels out and reaches a gateway and Public Bridleway sign. Go straight ahead onto the tarmac drive and up to the main road (B6106). Here turn right and cycle along to the shelter and bus stop at the end of Hollin Lane.

Section b-c

Both choices having rejoined, go into Hollin Lane and cycle up to the junction opposite the electricity pole, go left here. Cycle gradually uphill now for about 800m until, just before a farm, at the end of the track turn right through a field gate (with blue arrow on the post) and just before an electricity pole. Drop down before entering a large field and then follow the wall on the left up to a field gate on the sky-line. Go through the gate, ahead for about 10m before turning left on the grass track which then drops down. This passes a stone post with blue arrow on it, there being opencast workings to the left. Follow down until a wall is met (and a post with blue arrow) and then turn right and struggle uphill, aiming not to hit a gorse bush! The route soon levels out and then drops into a hollow with two bridle-gates and attendant wet patch.

Go through the gates and rise up on the walled track, then left and to another bridle-gate. Go through and then immediately right following the walled track, as the top is reached bear left onto a dirt track which leads through to the road. Turn left on the road, a bleak place on a wet day, and cycle along the straight stretch (Whitley Road) for about 850m to a road junction. Here turn left onto Lower Maythorne Lane for about 50m. Just after the small plantation on the right, turn right onto a walled track with gate. This track is boggy and wet in places. (*NOTE:* if you want to miss this out continue straight along Lower Maythorne Lane for about 1 km to a junction and then turn left, where the other route rejoins).

Cycle along the walled track, at a junction bearing to the right. Follow the track, over the brow, and begin to drop down towards Broadstone Reservoir. Go through the metal gate and then continue on a harder surface uphill to another metal gate and tarmac road beyond. Go left onto the tarmac road (single track). Cycle through the dwellings and then begin to drop, the tarmac having pot-holes at times and also muddy in places. A junction is eventually reached (the road just traversed being called Birds Nest Lane). At the junction go ahead onto the more major road with white lines in the centre. The road then rises gradually before dropping down a 14% hill with S-bends – this road being called Hogg Close Lane. Keep on until the main road (A616) is reached with Give Way signs and pub just to the left called Victoria Inn.

Section c-d

TAKING GREAT CARE, go straight across here onto Bedding Edge Road and cycle along for about 400m. A bridle route is off to the right just past a house and yard, and there is a Public Bridleway sign. (*NOTE:* you could cheat here and go straight along the road to the junction with the B6106 where the route described comes in opposite). Go through the gate and then follow left to another gate. Go through and then cycle along with a wall on the right to another gate near electricity poles. Go through this and go straight ahead, between two walls, and parallel to the electricity lines (there is a full wall on the left). Pass under the electricity lines on a sunken track and to another gate. Go through and then follow first ahead and then swinging down to the left to another bridle-gate.

Go through this, at the end of a length of broken wall (about 10m) go left for some 10-20m before swinging right onto a sunken track dropping downhill. Follow this rough track down to the bottom where there are a footpath sign and old buildings in the vicinity (Ox Lee). Go through the gap in the wall at the signs and drop onto the track ahead in the bottom. Take the track, through the gateposts with large wet area, keeping the buildings on the right. Go through a hollow before rising on the track which is paved with gritstone where the old vehicle wheels would have gone. Go up a gully (more like a stream bed) and to a gate. Go through the gate and onto the walled cinder track.

Follow the track which eventually begins to drop (muddy in places) and reaches a tarmac road with Public Bridleway sign – the track just used is called Ox Lee Lane. Go left here onto Bent Road which rises to a Stop sign at a junction near some houses and a post box. Go straight across here onto Law Slack Road, under a power line, passing a row of cottages on the right and rising all of the way to a junction at the top. Here go left onto what would be quite an exposed road in bad weather. The road rises, curves to the left over the summit and then descends to a road junction (B6106) at some houses at a Give Way sign and a telephone box. TAKING CARE, turn right, cycling past a Welcome to Barnsley notice and dropping downhill past the pub called the Foxhouse on the right. Some 200m past the pub, as the road bears left, take the bridleway which goes off on the right through a metal gate and Public Bridleway sign.

NOTE: the next bridleway poses a navigational problem – it depends on your abilities. It starts off very clearly-defined but the moorland section is hard to follow. On a misty day it is the case for a compass. To omit this section, continue straight down the B6106 for another 750m and then take the minor road on the right to Carlecotes. Follow this and, after some 1.5 km, the bridle route exits from the right.

Follow along the walled track on hard-core to the next bridle gate. Go through onto a muddy track, following a wall on the left. An area is soon reached with large pipes on the left. Go straight across here, following the wall on the left and down to a bridle gate. Go through this and then follow between the wall and stream down into the bottom where another bridle route comes in on the left. Turn right here, crossing the stream near where it goes through the wall and then follow the wall up. Follow the wall round to the left and keep rising, dropping down briefly to cross a stream. The path, although it can be followed, is indistinct and requires careful navigation. Keep climbing until, just before a gate and fence on the opposite side of the wall, veer away on a vague track.

Keep rising and moving away from the original wall, a wall will also be seen on the skyline. The wall on the skyline is gradually approached, the present track being about 100m off where the wall turns through a right angle. Keep in the same general line until parts of a fence area are seen, pass about 75m to the left of this. Soon a wide grass track is crossed and the present route begins to drop near a wall and the road can be seen ahead. Turn right and follow along the top side of the wall to the bridle gate. Go through this and then turn left in front of a small quarry face and to a bridle-way sign, bus stop and tarmac road.

Turn right onto the road and then drop down, round bends and through the few houses that form Townhead. Continue, past a road junction, and then drop towards Dunford Bridge. Slightly right can be seen the earthworks of the dam of Winscar Reservoir. Descend into Dunford Bridge, past the site of the former station and an access point onto the former railway line (the Trans-Pennine Trail).

Section d-a

Cross over the bridge, old tunnel entrances on the right, and the Stanhope Arms on the left. Then, you begin the hard pull up out of Dunford Bridge. The road begins to level near a Warning Sheep sign. A picnic site is passed on the left and then in about another 650m there is a Public Bridleway sign pointing off to the left. (On the right, is a ventilation shaft of the old tunnel).

NOTE: this bridle route can pose a navigational problem – it again depends on your abilities. To omit it, continue along the tarmac road for another 1.2 km to the junction with the A628 – an unpleasant road. Turn right for Langsett and then after 1.5 km the bridle route comes in from the left.

Take the bridle route which requires attention to navigation. It can be followed on the ground and there is a series of wooden posts with vestiges of blue paint at the top denoting the route. Follow these through occasional wet area and drop down to Uppermost Clough which feeds Upper Windleden Reservoir on the left. Cross this and take the track opposite, bearing left towards the railings. As the railings are approached follow round, with them on the left. After the best part of 100m, veer right, away from the railings and drop down to the stream at a point some 100m out from the railings in the bottom. The track climbs the opposite bank and up to a

Upper Windleden Reservoir (near Fidddlers Green)

fence post with bridle gate. It is a fair struggle up here! Go through the gate and then bear right; a larch tree is ahead, go for this and descend on to the obvious track with a stone wall and turn right.

Follow this track as it rises, crossing over the bridge on Woodland Clough and keep the steady uphill climb. It is quite tranquil here, save for the noise of the traffic on the major road ahead. The track is wet in places but is well defined. As the climb continues the traffic on the main road ahead will be seen near the skyline. Finally the exit bridle gate can be seen – an area known as Fiddlers Green. The last 20m to the gate is wet! At the main road (A628) you take your life into your hands – TAKE GREAT CARE. Turn left and head uphill, possibly using the verge. Alternatively try to wait for a lull in the traffic. Go past the parking sign to the lay-by. Continue over the crest and then just before a Warning Sheep sign, bear left over the kerb and to a field gate with Public By-way notice.

Go through the gate near the snow fences on to what is called the Snow Road. This is a pleasant change from the tarmac. The surface is now grass with underlying hard-core and is like this for almost the next two kilometres. It is a gradual and pleasant downhill gradient. Soon another field gate is encountered with Public By-way sign as the main road is again reached. Again, TAKING GREAT CARE, turn left onto the A628, immediately passing a public house called the Dog and Partridge. Cycle along the road for about 450m (there is no alternative) and then go right, watching the traffic, onto a Public Bridleway just before Delmont Grange.

Cycle down this walled track, on hard-core, through the bridle gate and onto the gateway with Boundary of Open Country sign. Just after passing under power lines, fork left on the Bridleway with attendant sign and head for a gate with stile and notice. Go through the gate and onto the walled grassy track known as Swinden Lane. Go over the brow, under the power lines and then through the gate. Continue along and then cross straight over a hard-core track near some more power lines. Go along to the next gateway where there is a notice Stock Grazing – Please Keep Dogs on Lead. Go through the gate and then turn left. Follow this track, through a gateway and to another junction.

Here turn left (as indicated by a blue arrow on a post) and head for the next gate and then following a wood on the right on what is called Badger Lane. Another bridle gate is soon reached and the wood proper is entered. Cycle along and then rise to the next junction (crossing over the Redmires to Holmbridge route at this point). Continue ahead on what is known as Brook House Lane, round the S-bend and up to the main road (A616) with Public Bridleway notices. TAKING GREAT CARE, go straight across here to the Bridle gate and the start of the route.

12. LONGDENDALE MEANDER

Distance: 13 km/8 miles

Route: Torside Information Centre – Rhodeswood Reservoir – Valehouse Reservoir – Bottoms Reservoir – Padfield – Tintwistle – Bottoms Reservoir – Valehouse Reservoir – Rhodeswood Reservoir – Torside Information Centre

Surface types: Tarmac, hard-core.

Suggested start: Torside Information Centre car park (SK068983).

Map: Dark Peak, 1:25000 or visitor leaflet.

Notes: For other routes visiting this area please see Woodhead Traverse and Snake to Crowden routes. There is a hostel and camp-site at Crowden. The area is surrounded by high moorlands and offers good walking and climbing. Please be courteous with all other users of the area.

Refreshment: Various pubs in Padfield/Hadfield and Tintwistle areas.

The Route

The routes around the Longdendale Reservoirs can be varied according to taste. They can be of a circular nature, i.e. returning to the starting point, or they can be end to end. The route described in this section is aimed at the family party and is of a circular nature.

On the Longdendale Trail (which goes from near Hadfield station to the Woodhead Tunnel) cyclists, walkers and the disabled share a gritstone route; horses use a separate parallel route separated by a ditch. The horse route has been seeded with grass, wild flowers and heather.

The Longdendale Trail is formed from part of the first railway link between Manchester and Sheffield – the Sheffield, Ashton under Lyne and Manchester Railway. For further information on the railway, see the Woodhead Traverse route.

The valley obviously also has a long history with water. The reservoirs and some of the catchment areas are now the property of North West Water. The water gathering grounds are some 6737 hectares (26 square miles) and take advantage of the heavy rainfall in this area. They provide some 125-130 megalitres (27.5-28.6 million gallons) of water per day for the eastern side of Manchester and environs.

The road through this valley (A628) was originally part of a turnpike road from Cheshire to Yorkshire which was authorised in 1731. However, salt has been carried through this area by pack horse from the Middle Ages but the trade was intensified in the 18th century. Some of the original routes can still be seen and ridden on. In addition some routes in the lower part of the valley are now under the reservoirs.

The Journey

Section a-b

Exit from the back of Torside Information Centre car park, through the gates and onto the Longdendale Trail, turn right and follow the south side of Torside Reservoir. Can you imagine the superb sights that were afforded to the passengers and train crews along here? After 1.1 km the site of Torside level crossing is reached. Go diagonal to the right here to where the track drops down and then immediately bear left – do not take the Pennine Way route. Go through the chicane and enter the next section of the trail. Cycle along here, on a general left-hand curve, following the southerly side of Rhodeswood Reservoir with scenic views and Bramah Edge up on the left.

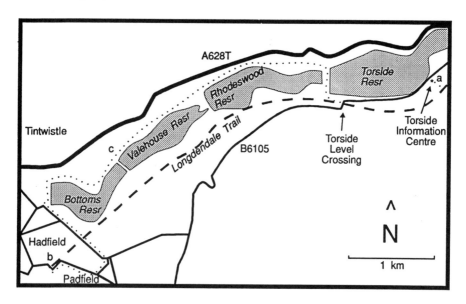

Travel here on a gently falling gradient. Valehouse Reservoir is soon passed and then Bottoms Reservoir, where you may see water skiing and a ski ramp with the reservoir name on it. Just before the next over-bridge, the footpath/cycle and horse routes transpose. Pass under Padfield Main Road and then the end of the trail is reached in just over 400m.

Compensation water outlet below Bottoms Reservoir

Section b-c

At the end of the trail go through the exit, looking ahead to Hadfield station – the present end of the railway from Manchester. Go through the small car parking area and to the road with attendant sign for the Longdendale Trail. NOW TAKE CARE. Turn left on to the road and pass underneath the bridge and follow the road round to the left and into Platt Street. Go through the signs for Padfield and then follow the road as it swings right and climbs.

Go left at the first road on the left (Bush Street). Climb here through the houses, passing a school set back on the left and then a Methodist chapel also on the left followed by a pub on the right. At the end of this road turn left into Padfield Main Road and drop downhill, crossing the trail by a bridge and then passing a Padfield sign. As the built up area is reached, this road turns sharp left; at this point go straight ahead onto a narrow walled road, which drops steeply. Go down here (Goddard Street), taking care with braking – this is a one-way street. At the bottom of the hill, just after the wooden fencing on the left and the two-way traffic sign (but before the junction with a main road) turn right onto a hard-core track. Then, go through the iron gate with a concessionary notice showing the route to Crowden.

Cycle along here as the track rises gradually, keeping the metal railings on the left, then swing left across the dam of Bottoms Reservoir. The track now crosses a bridge over the reservoir overflow channel and rises to the right and eventually to a large iron gate. Exit onto the tarmac near the North West Water workshops and then bear right for Bottoms Water Park and drop down on the walled road over the 'sleeping policemen'. Pass the car park entrance on the right and the quarry on the left where there are the remains of many stone blocks. When eventually the road swings to the right (heading across Valehouse Reservoir embankment), take the gated route on the left – a concessionary route to Crowden.

Follow along this tarmac track, with Valehouse Reservoir on the right. In just over 1 km a water board house is passed on the right, with the dam of Rhodeswood Reservoir ahead. The road then passes over a bridge where a water ladder can be seen on the left. Follow the road, rising up and round the hairpins to the gate at the top. Go through, turn left and over the bridge and then immediately right to the bridle gate.

Section c-a

Go through the bridle gate with notice: Concessionary Horse Route and Footpath to Crowden. Follow the hard-core track; the main A628 is up on left, with the rock face of Tintwistle Knarr Quarry higher up still. The track meanders along the northern side of Rhodeswood Reservoir, eventually dropping down over a bridge and then rising up to the gate beyond next to the woodland.

Go through the gate and then drop down on the tarmac surface, passing a house on the right. Follow the hard-core track as it swings right and over the dam of Torside Reservoir. At the end of the dam, go through the gateway and follow the tarmac track as it swings left and rises to meet the B6105 after about 250m and some gritstone setts. This is Torside level crossing again. Go across here, to the right, and onto the paved area and through the chicanes onto the Longdendale Trail again, the circle is now complete. Cycle along here, following Torside Reservoir for about 1.1 km, reversing the route described earlier. Turn left and return to the car park at Torside Information Centre.

13. LOW BRADFIELD TO HAYFIELD

Distance: 36 km/22.5 miles

Route: Low Bradfield – Damflask Reservoir – Ughill – Moscar Cross – Ladybower Reservoir – Thornhill – Aston – Hope Cross – Clough Farm – Edale – Upper Booth – Jacob's Ladder – Hayfield (Sett Valley Trail)

Surface types: Tarmac, hard-core, stone and grass.

Suggested start: Low Bradfield Car Park (SK262920).

Map: Dark Peak 1:25000, Peak District Tourist Map or Sheffield and Huddersfield (Sheet 110)

Notes: There are various other places to park at the rood side or lay-bys but these are not generally designated as such. This route links with Redmires to Holmbridge, Rowsley to Edale, Edale to Langsett, Edale Round, Chinley Churn and Rowarth Round routes. The Sett Valley Trail at Hayfield will also allow links to routes passing through Birch Vale. There is a Youth Hostel at Edale.

Refreshment: Ladybower Inn, Yorkshire Bridge, The Ramblers and Nags Head (Edale), various hostelries and refreshment in Hayfield.

The Route

This route provides a crossing of the Peak National Park from east to west. The route starts at Low Bradfield and visits the reservoirs of Damflask and Ladybower before crossing into the Edale Valley. There are alternatives on some sections if the weather is bad. Be extremely careful on the following sections in inclement weather: Ughill to Moscar Cross, Aston to Clough Farm and Upper Booth to Hayfield.

The route finishes in Hayfield at the car park for the Sett Valley trail, an old railway route which has been turned into a trail. It is open for walkers, horse riders and bicycle riders and can be followed to New Mills (almost). Other routes in this book visit this area or cross the trail, the present route can therefore be extended – see additional suggestions near the end of this book. This line was built for the Midland and Central Joint Railway Company and opened to traffic in 1868. The traffic consisted of both passengers and freight. The line was closed in 1970.

Be careful on the roads as some can become quite busy on good summer days, especially weekends and bank holidays.

The Journey

Section a-b

Bear left out of the car park and cycle along to the triangle, bear left here into Fairhouse Lane. Follow to the junctions and then left over the bridge (Smithy Bridge Road) for Low Bradfield and Worrall. On reaching the small garage on the right, go right as for Loxley. Follow this narrow road, initially close to Dam Flask reservoir. The road then rises to a road junction and 'Give Way' sign. Turn right here for Loxley, past another road junction, for about 1 km. As this junction is approached, turn right on a triangle and then go right onto the main road (B6076) for Dungworth.

The road now goes across Damflask Dam; on the left are the outlet sluices. Follow the road and continue along the other side, go past a junction and then fork left at the next, signed for Ughill. Go up here for about 600m and then take a left-hand road, still signed for Ughill and Strines. Rise to the summit and then begin a descent towards a wooded valley. At the road junction at the bottom, turn right (Strines and Derwent Valley) and cycle into Ughill.

Keep straight on here (for Strines and Derwent Valley), keeping Ughill Hall and Farm on the right. Leave Ughill, past a turn for Platts Farm and going uphill. The road eventually reaches the brow and turns to the left; a conifer woodland is passed on the right. About 100m past this woodland there is the choice of routes.

Section b-c

ROUTE 1: Not for bad weather unless experienced. Go left by a lonely tree and follow the walled track through to a gateway. Go through this and continue rising, keeping a wall on the right. Another wall comes in from the left and the walled track swings right. Follow this gradually uphill – quite a pleasant route in good weather, not so good in the face of a south westerly gale!

The walled route moves out into open moorland, there being little shelter from the elements. Pass through a gateway and note the ornate gate post here in the middle of nowhere. After about 1.8 km from leaving tarmac the track begins to drop and another gate is reached. Pass through and begin the descent, past another bridle route coming in from the left, to Moscar Farm. Keep straight ahead here, through two gateways and rising to a junction with waymark stone just to the left. Go left here and follow the route past Moscar Lodge to the main A57 and turn right, route 2 joins from the right after 250m. BE CAREFUL ON THIS MAIN ROAD.

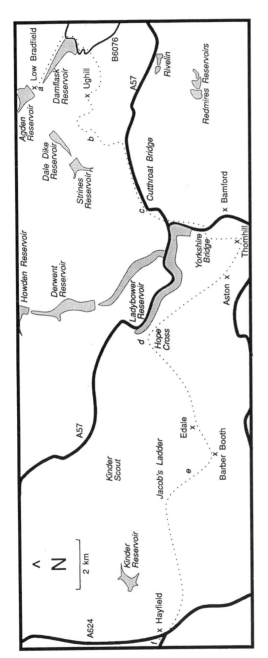

ROUTE 2: Keep on the tarmac road, dropping down past two right-hand turns until a road junction is reached just past a gas sub-station. Turn left and follow down to the A57, route 1 joins here.

Section c-d

After about 500m from the Strines road junction and immediately after Cutthroat Bridge, go left through the bridle gate. Follow the track for almost 50m and then bear to the left and follow the fence on the left, parallelling the power lines on the right.

Follow along here to a gate. Pass through this, over the stream and follow with a woodland on the left, ahead on the skyline is Win Hill. Drop down, always keeping towards the wall on the left, to another gate and Nature Reserve sign. Go through the gate and then down to the A57 and the Ladybower Inn. Note the tribute to 617 Squadron on the Inn sign. Take care, go right onto the A57 and follow down to the road junction, turn left on the B6013 for Bamford.

Cycle along here for some 650m, past the reservoir, the Ladybower Dam and the Yorkshire Bridge pub on the right. After the houses on the right, turn right immediately past the post box and signposted Thornhill. Drop downhill past the 'Unsuitable for Heavy Vehicles' notice and to Yorkshire Bridge at the bottom, cross over the River Derwent and turn left. Follow along this road, over the undulations and twists and turns, past a car park and then rise into Thornhill. Swing first to the right and then to the left. Coming out of this bend, there is a road junction just before a telephone box. Turn right here onto the road with 'Unsuitable for Motors' sign. Follow up here, past a chapel on the left and exit from the village.

Cycle along the narrow hedge-lined tarmac road, admiring the views to the left, marred only by the cement works. Continue along here until there is a farm on the left and then a road junction. Go straight across into Aston Lane and drop downhill. Pass the white house on the left, rise and then pass a post box on the left before dropping and entering a left-hand curve. As the road swings to the right, take the narrow tarmac lane that goes off to the right with sign for Win Hill and Hope Cross.

Climb up here past Kings Haigh Farm and then to Edge Farm. As Edge Farm is approached, go left in front of the wall onto a hard-core surface and rise to a gate. Pass through the gate and continue the gradual rise, bearing slightly right at one point, and keeping a stone barn on the right. Through the gate next to the barn and continue the rise on a walled section. Ahead are Lose Hill, Back Tor and the ridge to Mam Tor. The wall on the right swings away but keep on in the same general line on what can be discerned as a grass track. Go over the brow and drop to the signpost. Go straight ahead, through the gate posts and continue along under the plantation on the bridleway. Eventually a wall joins on the right; follow this to the next gate.

Go through this and then into more open terrain, continuing on the grass track. Slightly left are Hope, Castleton and the cleft that forms the Winnats Pass. Follow the grassed track, bearing right, with good views into the Edale Valley. Pass through three broken walls and gateposts before the track rises more steeply, finally reaching a junction. Turn left here and begin a gradual descent. Ahead is Derwent Edge and the strange rocky summits of Crook Hill. The track gradually draws closer to the woodland on the right. Follow this, then descend through a broken wall line and follow the track as it veers away from the woodland.

Drop down to a gateway where an old Roman Road is joined. Go through the gate and then along to the next gate where there is an old Guide Post on the right (Hope Cross) with markings for Sheffield, Hope, Edale and Glossop. Go through the gate and continue up to the gateway on the skyline.

Section d-e

Turn left and then follow the bridleway westwards, go through the gate and then head downhill on what at times is a multiplicity of grooves caused by endless erosion. Drop down and cross the stream – Jaggers Clough – and through the gate, bearing right. After a 100m or so follow the hairpin to the left and go uphill on a stepped section – repaired by the National Trust. Go over the summit and then start to drop down to Clough Farm, go through the gate and then follow down to the tarmac road. Turn right here and follow the valley road for 1.1 km, past the YHA sign and finally to the Edale road and car park on the right.

❏ *NOTE:* There is a right turning into Edale village. In the village is a shop, post office and pubs plus a National Park Information Centre. Edale is the start of the Pennine Way but there are NO cycle routes out of the village itself, ONLY footpaths. The railway station is also up this road.

Continue straight along the valley road for Barber Booth, passing Waterside caravan and camping site and then Upper Booth on the right. Follow the main road round over the bridge and then turn immediately right onto the road with *No Through Road* sign and fingerpost to Upper Booth and Lee House and continuing as Bridleway to Hayfield. Cycle along the tarmac, under the railway bridge, past Barber Booth car park, Highfield Farm camping and caravans, eventually reaching the houses and telephone box that call themselves Upper Booth. Continue, dropping down over a bridge and then rising again (following signs for Jacob's Ladder), finally coming to a gate with National Trust sign for Lee Farm. Go through this and continue along to the farm. Here the tarmac ceases. Go straight through the farmyard, past the information shelter on the left and through the gate.

NOTE: It is worth having a look in the information shelter as it has been refurbished as a byre and has information posters on the wall.

Section e-f

Continue along the hard-core track which deteriorates to stone/earth just after a bridge. Continue along here, through several gates, looking up to the skyline where Edale Rocks, and to the right, Noe Stool, can be seen. Continue until the gate is reached at the packhorse bridge, and cross the river by either the bridge or the ford. This can be an idyllic place on a sunny day. Once over the stream, turn to the left and follow the walled track – the old packhorse route. DO NOT take the cycle up the steps of Jacob's Ladder. Follow up, round the hairpin and eventually reach the top of Jacob's Ladder where there is a cairn and footpath sign and possibly time for a short rest. Turn here and continue on the stony surface.

Looking towards Jacob's Ladder

The track first rises, then levels slightly before a steep uphill pull on a surface of gritstone blocks. On the right is a gatepost halfway up this section with bench mark towards the bottom. Continue to the top and rest awhile on a newly-built low wall topped with gritstone flags. Admire the scenery from here. The route now continues up, curving slightly until a gate is reached, which you go through and continue on the obvious track.

DO NOT GO OFF ONTO THE MOORS FROM HERE, THE ACCESS IS ONLY FOR PEDESTRIANS.

Drop down before the very last bit of ascent on this leg to the gateposts at the mediaeval Edale Cross. Start to drop down now with views of Hayfield and beyond to Stockport and Manchester. Keep dropping now, keeping a gritstone wall on the right. Cross over Stony Ford, eventually reaching another gate, just before which a bridle route goes off to Glossop on the right. Pass through the gate. On reaching a four-way signpost, continue straight ahead, signed for Hayfield. Continue down to the next gate. Having passed through this veer right, passing over a bridge and attaining a tarmac surface. Head towards the houses and going to the right of the trees. Pass the houses at Coldwell Clough (dated 1804).

This is a pleasant drop down here on a tarmac surface. As two gates are approached go to the left-hand one, pass through, cross a bridge and then rise uphill. A bridle route sign is then passed and in another 100m another one. Take this second bridle track to continue across an open field, eventually coming to a bridle gate in a wall. Go through this and then take the lower track which goes straight ahead with the trees on the left (do not go uphill on the walled track). Follow this round to the left and begin the descent for Hayfield. The track has some rough sections on it in places – rocks and tree roots. Pass a house on the left and then a camp site will be seen ahead. Keep following the track down and round to the left again. Just keep going and eventually you reach a bridle gate near two wooden electricity poles with mounted transformer. Go through the gate (with a notice for Stones House Farm), soon being joined by a footpath from the right. Continue alongside the River Kinder, a rough tarmac surface beginning near some houses. Continue along the road, bearing right at a junction, past more houses and then onto a better and wider tarmac surface.

Follow down to the Give Way sign. Go right here and to the Stop sign. Refreshments etc are to the right. For the route, turn left and go down to the by-pass, BE CAREFUL HERE. Turn right onto the main road as for the Sett Valley Trail. Cycle downhill to the junction (about 40m) and bear left for the Trail. Pass the Kinder Lodge pub on the right and then immediately after The Spinnery turn right into Station Road and into the car park area.

14. MARPLE TO CHINLEY

Distance: 19 km/12 miles

Route: Marple Station – Bottom's Hall – Mellor Cross – Rowarth – Matley Moor – Lantern Pike – Birch Vale – Moor Lodge – Throstle Bank – Chinley Station

Surface types: Tarmac, hard-core, earth.

Suggested start: Marple Station.

Map: Dark Peak 1:25000 and Touring Map and Guide 4, Peak District (1 inch to 1 mile).

Notes: This route can be linked into the Chinley Churn or Rowarth Round routes or, by cycling down the Sett Valley trail to Hayfield, linked into routes for Edale and beyond.

Refreshment: Norfolk Arms (Marple), Moorfield Arms (near Rowarth), The Squirrels (Chinley).

The Route

The route goes from Marple Station to Chinley Station and is a linear route. It leads from the urban area of Marple through gritstone country to Rowarth, over moorland (Lantern Pike) to Birch Vale and then along old county roads to Chinley.

Marple is where the Peak Forest and Macclesfield canals meet and they then cross the River Goyt to the north of the town by means of 16 locks and an aqueduct.

Lantern Pike is a moorland hilltop with views to N, SW and E. It was given in 1949 as a memorial to Edwin Royce, a past president of the Manchester Ramblers' Federation.

The Journey

Section a-b

From Marple Station exit onto the main road and turn left downhill, taking great care, passing St. Martyns Church on the left. Go down to the light just on the bridge exit and then turn right (TAKING GREAT CARE) in front of the Norfolk Arms.

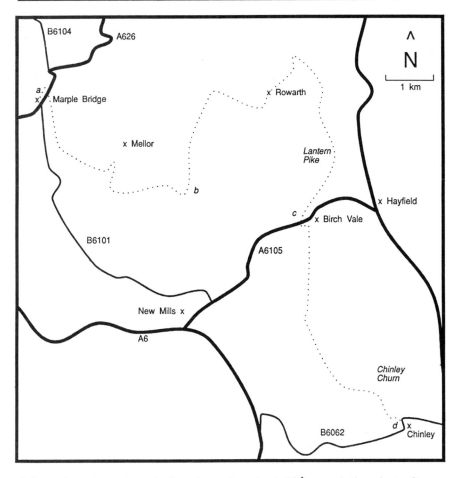

Follow along here through the shops 'for about 200m, and then just after a pharmacy on the right, turn right into Low Lead Road. Drop down over a couple of bridges on what has now become a rougher surface and then rise past the houses and cottages. The track continues past various dwellings, a footpath sign on the left, before dropping down as a fenced lane. As the bottom is approached there are road signs on the left informing of the change from Low Lea Rd to Bottoms Mill Road. Continue with trees on either side to the junction.

Here turn left as for Roman Lakes and Goyt Way into what is called Lakes Rd. Follow this for about 200m to the next junction, here continue straight ahead, passing to the left of Bottom's Hall and Old Hall Farm. Just before the farm note the attractive stone arch of a bridge over the stream on the right. Continue up and past the farm on the walled and stony track. This track now twists and turns as it climbs, look over to the right and the Roman Lakes can be seen. The track then turns into the hill and follows a small stream on the right. After a right-hand bend the track begins to level out and straighten with the semblance of a paved path on the right made from gritstone blocks.

Continue along here until a tarmac track is reached, just after a compound on the right full of wooden pallets. There is a parking area on the left for the Scout Camp and the road being followed is called Neills Way, signposted for Mellor and Cobden Edge. Continue along here past and through Mellor and Towncliffe Golf Club. The road rises and then swings left and over a brow, here turn right through the small car park just before the 30 mph signs. The road contours along the hill side through golf country (watch out for white missiles), before departing near a broken wall and dropping downhill past a house on the left.

Shortly after this bear left at the junction and rise, through stone gate posts, the track being hedged on the left and fenced on the right. Pass Lillybank Farm on the left and then just before a gateway there is a bridle path sign pointing to the left and going up between the houses. Follow this up the steps, it being wiser to push than try to ride! Follow the narrow track steeply uphill, heading initially towards a

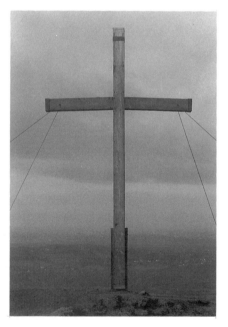

telegraph pole. The track then swings right through a pair of gateposts, go straight ahead here towards another telegraph post on the skyline (do NOT turn left). It is a bit of a struggle to obtain this post, but shortly after this muddy track leads onto a tarmac surface. Here, head up and away from the houses towards the cross on the skyline, passing Bull Hill Farm on the right.

When the tarmac road goes sharply left, go straight ahead onto an earthen track just to the right of a renovated house with large church-like window frames. It is worth a detour on foot to the cross. The notice on it tells us that it was erected by Marple and District Council of Churches, 27 March 1970 – but not why. There are good views on a clear day, looking way across Marple, Stockport, Manchester and beyond. Continue up the walled lane until it bears left and then levels out over the summit; look to the right to see if you spot the trig point in the heather. The track now descends to a junction where there is an old caravan; turn right here. Follow this narrower walled track, dropping slightly past a house and then to a crossroads. Here turn left and follow over the brow by a small reservoir called Broadhurst Edge. Continue along this track for another 500m or so until a junction is encountered with tarmac roads.

Section b-c

Go straight across here onto a tarmac road called Shiloh Lane, BE CAREFUL as you cross Moor End Rd, it's like a race track at times! Drop down under power lines, pass the Moorfield Arms and then shortly after turn right for Rowarth. Follow this road down for about 850m and then turn left for Rowarth. Go round the bends, pass a car park on the right and then enter the hamlet. Continue straight through, past a junction where there is a house called Anderton House and dated 1797. The surface deteriorates and you exit through the 30 mph signs. At a junction, keep ahead onto the road with dead-end notice and go uphill.

After about 250m a signpost indicates a bridleway bearing right through a gate set at an angle to the road. Go through the gate onto an earthen track and then descend, through a ford with signposts and continue up on the muddy walled track until a gate is reached leading onto tarmac. Cycle up the tarmac road, passing Ivy Cottage as the track swings left-ish. Continue until there is a large solitary tree on the left with a footpath sign beyond. Turn right here onto a walled track with hard-core surface. Follow this up and then through the gate as it veers right and continue on the initially walled track.

The wall on the left soon turns away, but you follow the wall on the right, choosing the route carefully. A bridle gate is soon encountered, after passing through and an initial muddy section, the surface improves as Matleymoor Farm is approached. Swing round the farm and then swing right on the hard-core track, dropping down, making good going, past Bullshaw Farm and then rise again to a junction.

Here there is a multi-way signpost. Go through the bridle gate on the right and then veer left through 60 degrees and head as for Birch Vale. Head towards the top corner of the field – the route is obvious on the ground but may be difficult in snow conditions. Cross the field on the grass/mud track and rise to the bridle gate with No Motorcycles notice. Go through here onto National Trust land called Lantern Pike. The track is initially stony but becomes muddy as it swings left and follows the wall with bridleway notice. It is worth leaving the bikes and making a detour on foot to the top of Lantern Pike for the views. Otherwise continue with the wall on the left, over the summit and then dropping gradually with heather on the right. Keep dropping; Hayfield is on the left, a TV mast ahead and then, as the track veers right, there are views down into Birch Vale.

Keep dropping, passing through the gate as you exit from National Trust land. Follow the track down with wall on the left, curve round to the right, passing between two gateposts, the track is now walled and the surface improves. Pass the cottages and drop down for another 300m to the tarmac road at some more cottages. Here go right and then almost immediately left on to a small tarmac lane with bridleway sign and notice stating No Motorcycles. Continue down here for another 300m to a hairpin; go ahead and through the bridle-gate onto a walled and earthen track above the trees. This track soon begins to drop and becomes stony, eventually reaching a cobbled surface before the tarmac road below. Turn left here, taking care, past a notice saying Spier Bottom and over the River Sett.

Section c-d

Immediately after the bridge turn right onto a tarmac track with bridleway sign. Follow along with the river on the right. At a blue gateway with *GWL* on it, leave the river and branch left onto a narrow and sometimes muddy track. Rise up, veering left, over the Sett Valley Trail and continue up a very muddy track with a wall coming in on the right. Climb steeply, go through a gap in a stone wall, and then bear left onto a gravel track into the road. Here turn left, taking care, and follow for about 200m, immediately after the row of houses on the right turn right just before what looks like a small converted chapel and cycle uphill, doubling back on oneself.

Follow this tarmac road up as it swings left, passing Birch Vale quarry and continue the uphill drag. After about 800m the track surface deteriorates but still rises over a summit and drops to Moor Lodge and a junction. Here follow almost straight ahead on the walled track and climb again on a stony surface and reach another summit. Continue ahead on an almost level and wide section to another junction where a tarmac road (Laneside Road) comes in on the left; on the left is another bridle route up to Chinley Churn. Continue ahead here, dropping down and then up again, from where the track begins to level out.

Cycle along here (what is called Over Hill Rd), admiring views away to the right of New Mills, Whaley Bridge etc. Eventually a tarmac road is met on a hairpin bend. Go left and continue on the higher section. Follow the road round, passing the bottom of another bridle route leading on to Chinley Churn and Throstle Bank Farm.

The road now begins to drop and at one point you can see railway viaducts just outside Chapel-en-le-Frith. Pass a large antenna tower on the left, enjoying the downhill stretch. Eventually habitation is met with attendant 30 mph signs. Continue until ahead there is an Unsuitable for Motor Vehicles sign, here bear right over the railway bridge and immediately to a road junction. Go across here into Green Lane, passing in front of the pub called The Squirrels, and then turn right into Station Rd and cycle along until the footway into the station is encountered.

15. MARSDEN ROUND

Distance: 28 km/17.5 miles

Route: Marsden – Standedge Cutting – Diggle – Castleshaw Reservoirs – Denshaw – Readycon Dean Reservoir – A640 – Bradshaw – Marsden

Surface types: Tarmac, hard-core, earth

Suggested start: Marsden (Tunnel End) but has limited parking, Marsden Railway Station

Map: Sheffield and Huddersfield (Sheet 110) and Manchester (Sheet 109). Part of OS Touring Map and Guide 4, Peak District (1 inch to 1 mile).

Notes: There should be no navigational problems on any part of this route. The high ground is, however, very exposed and the weather conditions can be severe. There is a bunkhouse about 1 km past Standedge Cutting on the Diggle side.

Refreshment: Tunnel End Inn, The Railway (plus various in Marsden not on route), Carriage House, Great Western, Floating Light, Diggle Hotel, Junction Inn (Denshaw), Rams Head, Buckstones Inn, Nont Sarah's Hotel, Rose and Crown, The Swan (Marsden)

The Route

This route starts in Marsden in Yorkshire, and crosses over into Lancashire before returning. Marsden is a typical small mill town in the Colne Valley where wool means wealth. Marsden stands at the end of tunnels which took two forms of transport across the Pennines, first the canal and then the railway. The road link goes over the top. The area therefore has a historical connection with trans-Pennine links.

Before the canal tunnel was opened, all cargo travelling by canal had to be transhipped at Uppermill and Marsden and conveyed by pack horse across the Pennines. The tunnel construction took 16 years and was opened in April, 1811. The tunnel is longer than the railway tunnels and is some 4.95 km (3 miles 135 yards) long. Within the tunnel there are several wide places to allow barges to pass. The last cargo boat is reputed to have travelled through the tunnel in 1921 and the tunnel was finally closed in 1944 by an Act of Parliament. As there is no tow-path through the tunnel the barges were propelled by men lying on their backs on the barge and pushing against the tunnel walls. There was a team of two who were known as 'Leggers' and a typical passage time was 4 hours. The barge horses were taken over the top by Boat Lane, part of which is used by the cycle route – see later.

The canal (Huddersfield Narrow Canal) begins at a junction with the Huddersfield Broad Canal at Aspley Basin. From the Colne Valley to Tunnel End at Marsden the canal rises some 133m (436ft) using 42 locks. The canal emerges at Diggle (also visited on the cycle route) and then drops by 102m (334ft) through 32 locks.

Standedge railway tunnels consist of three bores, two early single track tunnels and a later double track tunnel. The first railway tunnel for the Huddersfield and Manchester Railway was begun in 1846 and took two years to construct. A second tunnel was started at the same time but was abandoned for some 20 years before completion in 1871. A third tunnel was required because of an increase in rail traffic was begun in 1890 and finished in 1894. It is now the only tunnel in use and forms part of the main Leeds to Liverpool line. This tunnel is 4.89 km (3 miles, 66 yards) long. The canal tunnel was used by railway engineers for carrying materials and is connected to the rail tunnel by adits.

The Roman fort at Castleshaws was built as an outpost on the route from Chester to York and occupied some 1.3 ha (3.2 acres) during the Agricolan period. About 5 years after it was built it seems to have been abandoned and left deserted until early in the second century AD. A small fort was then built with an area of about 0.26 ha (0.65 acres).

The Journey

Section a-b

From Tunnel End: Cycle up out of the car park and turn right at the end onto the road opposite Tunnel End Inn. Follow the road along and then right over the railway and canal bridge and to the station. Go past the station and drop down on Station Road past a pub called The Railway. As the road then swings to the left, turn right going up past the Church of St Bartholomew's and to the main road (A62), TAKING GREAT CARE, cross straight over into Old Mount Road and begin a struggle uphill! Down on the left is the dam of Butterley Reservoir and the golf course. There are plenty of seats along here for the weary. The views to the moors begin to open out, soon the road drops to a junction, here turn right. The road rises to the summit past a footpath stating Boat Lane before beginning to drop to the main road (on the right is the Carriage House).

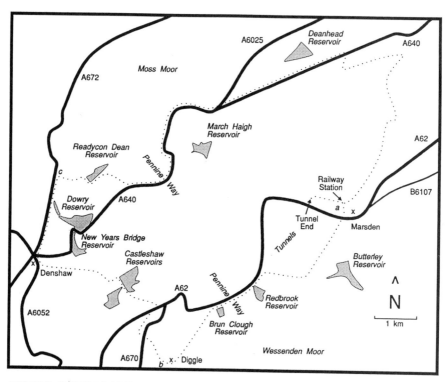

TAKING GREAT CARE, turn left onto the main A62 and rise gradually up past the pub called the Great Western and into Standedge Cutting with 'Saddleworth' sign, where there is a crawler lane. Go over the summit and then to the Pennine Way crossing with car park and Brun Clough Reservoir on the left. There is a variation here:

For the purist: follow along the fence of the reservoir, rising, (almost parallel to the road) and to a field gate, go through and then drop to the track below.

For the easy route: continue on the road to just past the reservoir and then turn left onto a track with metal gate. This is just before a road junction and a pub called the Floating Light.

Follow the main track to a hollow just past a house on the left and where there is a footpath sign – DO NOT follow the obvious track uphill. Turn right at the footpath sign (this is a Bridle Path) and follow the wall on the right below the spoil heaps and capped ventilation shaft. Follow this wall as the route drops, across a stream, and keep following the wall through to a bridle gate at Diggle Edge Farm with signpost. Go through the gate onto tarmac, go left and drop down right, keeping the buildings on the left and back onto hard-core at a metal gate. Continue on the fenced/walled track and keep dropping, far down below you can see where the railway lines and canal have emerged from the tunnel. Keep dropping and the track soon reaches the back of Diggle Hotel. Go straight through the car park to the road where there are *Bridleway* and *Boat Lane* signs.

As something interesting to do: immediately before the hotel car park, take the track off on the right and drop down over the tunnel mouth. You can now look down onto the railway lines and site of the former Diggle Station. Looking down the track, you can see where the canal tunnel exits. Follow the track round and attain the road at the other side of the bridge.

Section b-c

Turn right out of the Diggle Hotel car park and cross over the bridge, follow the road round to the left until just before a telephone box and then double back on the right onto Harrop Green Lane. This rises steeply into Harrop Green, keeping to the left, after which drop down to the left and to a cross roads. Go straight across onto Carr Lane, follow round to the right before rising steeply to the left and up onto the A670. Turn right here for about 50m and then go left onto an unmade track which rises. Follow round the bends, first left and then right and onto a better surface and to a cross roads near some sheds. Here turn right onto a wider track and follow up over the summit where there is a small TV antenna and then drop down to the main A62 (the road just traversed being called Harrop Edge Lane).

TAKING GREAT CARE, turn right onto the main road for some 150m before bearing left onto a minor tarmac road which drops down towards houses. After just over 100m and a post box turn left onto a narrow road between the houses. Follow this round various bends, past the remains of the Roman Fort and to the Reservoir. Bear right and cross over the dam between the reservoirs on tarmac. At the end turn left onto a hard-core track and along to a gate just before a house. Through the gate and then right, through another gate and rise uphill on a walled lane – known as Gate Lane. Follow this until, eventually, a gate is reached with a multi-way signpost. Continue ahead as for Denshaw.

The track first drops before rising on a wet section – and just before the summit on the left is a trough from where the water comes. Cycle along on a gently descending gradient with New Years Bridge Reservoir way down on the right. Soon a gate is reached and you're on a tarmac surface (known as Ox Hey Lane). Continue ahead, being careful of any Vietnamese pot bellied pigs. Follow the road

Between Castleshaw and Denshaw

round various bends to the house with radio antennas, here turn right into Wham Lane and drop to the main road (A6052). TAKING CARE, turn right onto the main road and rise into Denshaw and a complex road junction with *Stop* and *Give Way* signs.

At this junction where there is a mini-roundabout, TAKE GREAT CARE, turn right to go in front of the Junction Inn onto the A672 for Halifax (Ripponden Road). Continue past the Rams Head for about 300m from where there are some gates on the right.

Section c-a

Go through the gates and continue on the well-defined hardcore/sandy track heading away from the main road. If it is clear, you can see Readycon Dean Brook down on the right. All I saw in the fog were lots of four legged woolly animals thinking I had food for them! Continue along to Readycon Dean Reservoir, swing right over the dam and then go immediately left. This track now follows a wall on the left which soon ceases. The track now bears right and climbs. At a minor junction, keep ahead, rising uphill. The track gently descends until a gate is reached at road side with a Public Right of Way sign. There is now some 7 km (just over 4 miles) of road work.

TAKING GREAT CARE, turn left onto the A640 and head towards Huddersfield. The road steadily rises, past the crossing of the Pennine Way and small car park (also a suitable end point) and swings first left and then right and starts a gentle descent with *Welcome to Kirklees* notice. Keep cycling on! Buckstones Inn and Restaurant is passed on the left just before some rock outcrops. At the road junction keep on the A640 as for Huddersfield (there is also a car parking area here). There are good views here ahead in clear weather. Keep dropping until immediately before Moorland Lodge and a pub (Nont Sarah's Hotel), turn right onto a hard-core track. Drop down on the track and then rise round to the left before passing a house on the right and the track becoming muddy in places. Ahead are two large radio masts, on the right views into the valley below.

Keep heading along the track which soon becomes tarmac at a junction. Keep straight ahead, past another junction and drop down on tarmac to another road (the road just ridden along is called Burnt Platts Lane). Turn right and at then at the next junction keep right on Laund Road. Follow this as it swings right and a fork is reached with a chapel-looking building in the apex. Bear left onto the No Through Road called Tyas Lane. This drops down very steeply, the tarmac changing to cobbles which are quite greasy in wet weather – take care! Keep on down to the bridge at the bottom where the cobbles cease.

Go over the bridge and then bear left on the track as it rises, over another cobble section. The track then goes up on the left to miss a small ravine (where the original track was). Keep climbing, various detours being made to miss bad patches. Eventually a tarmac road is reached. Keep straight uphill towards power lines and a radio mast and a crossroads, opposite a pub called the Rose and Crown (the road just used is called Scout Lane).

Go straight across onto Marsden Lane (with width prohibition notice), past the pub and then begin to drop with good views beyond. The road drops and drops and drops, a section is passed with cobbled centre section just before a hairpin to the left. Go down past a cream coloured house and parallel to the railway to a junction. Turn right here, under the bridge and then right just before a No Through Road sign. Keep cycling along above Sparth Reservoir and the canal. As the canal draws near, there is an access point on the left for a visit to the locks and basin.

Continue on the tarmac road, soon entering a built-up area, Cross over the canal and into Industrial Revolution scenery with mills and mill houses. At the road junction just after the United Church Marsden on the right, go right past a pub called The Swan, over the River Colne and head back for the station (and Tunnel End if applicable).

16. MATLOCK TO BUXTON

Distance: 35.5 km/22 miles

Route: Matlock – Jugholes – Winster – Elton – Dale End – Middleton – Parsley Hay – Hurdlow – Earl Sterndale – Harper Hill – Buxton

Surface types: Tarmac, hard-core, earth

Suggested start: Matlock, various car parks, station or Youth Hostel.

Map: White Peak 1:25000

Notes: The route is deliberately started at the centre of Matlock to cater for various start points in the vicinity. Buxton then forms a link onto other routes such as Buxton to Bollington, New Mills to Buxton and Buxton to Hathersage.

Refreshment: Matlock (various), Miners Standard (Winster), Jug and Glass, Duke of York (Elton), Parsley Hay, Royal Oak (Hurdlow), Quiet Woman (Earl Sterndale), various in Buxton.

The Route

This route goes from Matlock with its Youth Hostel and railway station, to Elton and its Youth Hostel, near the Youth Hostel at Youlgreave and through to the Youth Hostel at Buxton (or the railway station).

The route is entirely in the White Peak, so called because of the colour of the limestone. The journey goes from Matlock, up through the higher plateau area to Buxton, the highest market town in England. You pass through pleasant scenery and see eyesores of both past times – lead mining – and the present-day quarrying.

Part of the route uses the Tissington and High Peak Trails on former railway lines that were closed in the late 1960s. The last part of the route into Buxton skirts the edge of a large quarry and passes close to a mines research establishment, previously a munitions depot for the last war.

The Journey

Section a-b

From the roundabout in the centre of Matlock, take the direction of A6 Derby. Cross over the River Derwent and go straight ahead as the main road swings left. Rise to the left past the ornate buildings of the Royal Bank of Scotland on Snitterton Road. Cycle up here for about 275m, past the Kingdom Hall of Jehovah Witnesses and to just before the de-restriction signs. Turn left here onto a narrow road known as Salters Lane with a Single File Traffic sign. Go uphill here, turn sharp right at the entrance to Green Hills Farm and through the de-restriction signs. The road now becomes quite narrow and sunken in places – be wary of other traffic. As the road rises a notice is passed about blasting by the Tarmac Company. The road quickly gains height and eventually starts to level out with a radio mast on the right. The road then begins to drop, past several footpath signs and is now known as Nailor Lane.

The road eventually bears left to a junction. Turn right here and then after about 50m turn left onto a walled track known as Moorlands Lane. (You can cut the corner off if the small track is spotted on the right as the junction is approached). Cycle up here, rising gradually, passing a barn on the right. Some footpaths lead off this lane and bushes encroach. As the track enters out into a more open area, just before a ruined barn is reached on the left, bear right and follow along the track with fence on the left. This track swings round a huge mound of earth that has been quarried, past large metal gates and continue along until a junction is met.

Turn left for about 100m and then turn right into what is known as Blakemere Lane. Go down here, passing a small barn on the right and down to where, on the right, is a wetland area with reeds and water – known as Blakemere and an attractive site for a rest. Rise again, the spoil heaps in the fields being the remains of lead mining, to a tarmac road. There are now two possible routes

Route 1 (this is the easiest): turn right up the tarmac road (Bonsallmoor Lane) and follow to the road junction, here turn left onto Bonsall Lane.

Route 2 (for the adventurous): go straight over the tarmac and follow the track beyond, ignoring any possible turn-offs until the track veers sharply left, here turn right and go through a gate next to a squeezer stile onto the unsigned bridlepath. *(NOTE*: this is shown as a bridlepath on the definitive map yet the stiles have only been included in most places). Follow the wall on the right as it drops, through a

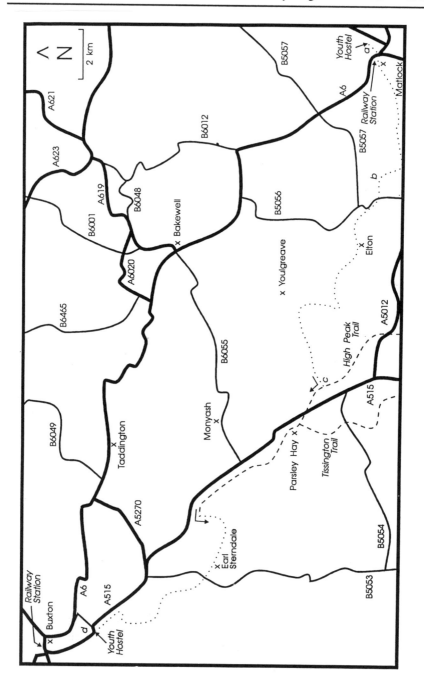

gap in a wall and then onto a metal gate. Go through this and then go past a solitary tree on the right and to the next wall – only a stile with large stone gatepost. Go through here and continue to follow the wall on the right, over which are spoil heaps left from lead mining. The next wall is broken but at the next one, a stile is encountered.

Go through another stile and then under power lines. As a metal gate is approached, go right through a stile and then bear left and head through a gap in a broken wall. Go to another stile just to the right of a pole on the second power line. Go through here and then follow a wall on the left, with power line, to the next stile, go through here. Continue following the power line to where it ceases and then over another stile. Go straight across the field to the next stile with pond down on the left. Go through here and continue on the trod, eventually reaching a gate and stile leading onto tarmac. Route 1 comes in from the right. Turn left.

Both routes, having rejoined, follow along Bonsall Lane, past two derelict barns and then a wetland area on the right. Drop down to a road junction. Although these roads appear quiet, be careful of the big quarry lorries.

Section b-c

Turn right onto the B5056 as for Bakewell. After about 100m fork left for Elton and Newhaven. (If desperate for a drink, go ahead to the Miners Standard, Winster). At the Give Way sign go straight over onto a walled track with hard-core surface. Go past a barn on the left; the track becomes sunken and drops – the strange rocks on the right are called Grey Tor. Drop down and straight over the farm track. Then rise past a dilapidated barn on the right and cycle along onto a pleasant wall and hedge-lined track.

When this reaches tarmac at a junction, turn left for Elton. Soon the 30 mph and village signs are reached. Cycle along through the houses, passing a *Youth Hostel 300yds* sign. The youth hostel is passed on the left just after a telephone box. Continue ahead, past All Saints Church, Elton on the right, it might be possible to find the Duke of York Inn on the left! At the junction keep on the main road which curves right as for Gratton and through the de-restriction signs. Cycle along this narrow, walled road through Dale End. At a junction just out of Dale End near a building (an old cheese factory), fork left and rise uphill.

The road goes over the summit and drops; at one point, rock outcrops are seen in a small dale on the right. The road drops past Smerrill Grange before a sharp right-hand bend where a bridle route to Long Dale goes off. Keep on the tarmac, soon rising over the brow – this is known as Weaddon Lane – and dropping into Middleton by Youlgreave by St Michael's Church and to a junction.

NOTE: if you go right here, Youlgreave is soon reached where there is a Youth Hostel. At Middleton, Roman coins and a bronze Fibula were found in AD 1843.

Turn left at the junction (as for Newhaven and Ashbourne) and cycle up Rake Lane on a 10% gradient through the trees of Rake Wood. Keep straight on at the next junction as for Newhaven and in a further 800m reaching a crossroads. Go straight across here (taking care) onto a road with *Unsuitable for Motors* sign. Cycle along on this rough tarmac surface, past the entrance to Mere Farm on what is known as Green Lane. After the barn on the right the surface degenerates into dirt/stone. The track rises through the trees and then drops down on a sometimes stony surface into a hollow where it can be wet and muddy at times. Rise out of here, noting the disturbed landscape and pits on the left with rock faces. The track levels and then descends again, the white building up ahead being a pub – the Jug and Glass which serves Real Ale! The route drops through the hollow and then rises to the left and soon to a junction with the Tissington and High Peak Trails. (If desperate, on a summer day, one could continue straight ahead for 400m and then along the main road for a drink at the Jug and Glass).

Section c-d

Turn right through the gates and follow the Trail which can be very busy in summer. A nature reserve at Blakemoor is passed through, going under the bridge with an old signal post just before it.

NOTE: Heather grows in this area, which is not usual on limestone. This area shows signs of mans disturbance and must have an acidic content.

After the bridge the track curves left into a cutting, heading for a short tunnel under the A515. On the tunnel is a crest for the Cromford and High Peak Railway with the date 1825. Go under the road and the final approach to the junction just south of Parsley Hay is being made. On reaching the junction bear right onto the other Trail. If you look back down onto the other trail, there is a spectacular cutting. Cycle the next few hundred metres to Parsley Hay where there is a cycle hire centre and refreshments.

Continue north along the trail from Parsley Hay, the surface is easy going and good time will be made.

NOTE: In just over 1 kilometre one reaches some farm buildings on the right, look to the either side of the trail here and you will see the original alignment of the railway. These had some severe curves that could not be negotiated by later rolling stock – hence the present alignment.

Carry on past the farm, under the bridge and then through the cutting. Just after the cutting, pass over a road bridge with fence railings, continue ahead and soon a car parking/picnic area is reached at Hurdlow. Continue along the trail, under the bridge and past the Royal Oak for about 2 km when a gate is reached at the end of the Trail. Go through and left into the walled lane. Rise here and then down onto a tarmac road, here go right. Go through the dip, under the power lines, over the summit and then to a road junction. Go right here and drop downhill. Take time to admire the views down on the left and Aldery Cliff.

Pass the entrance to Braemar Farm on the right and keep dropping through the 30 mph signs to the road junction and Earl Sterndale sign. Go right here and follow through the villages, passing a pub called the Quiet Woman on the left. Drop down through the de-restriction signs to the crossroads. Go straight ahead here (taking care) as for Dalehead and Axe Edge. Go past a white house and a cottage called Hatch-a-way. The road continues to rise, past a farm called Harley Grange and then, in about 1 km, follow the tarmac surface to the left (ignore any reference to bridle route). Follow the road for about another 800m with barbed-wire fence on the right, as it rises and then drops towards a hollow. As the hollow is approached the road bears right, just as this bend is left there is a bridle-gate with sign on the right.

Go through the bridle-gate and then follow the remains of the wall on the left up to a post on the skyline. Here there is another post ahead, soon after which a whole line of posts is followed, past a corner of a fence and then to a bridle-gate. Go through the gate and then turn left and follow down along the fence, the track at times showing signs of chatter. Look ahead here and see a quarry face and the buildings of High Peak College situated at about 375m (1230ft) above sea level, probably the highest college in the UK. When the fence finishes, follow the track as it bears right, over a shoulder of land and then dropping straight across a derelict railway siding and down to a bridle-gate at the side of an obviously disused railway line.

Go through the bridle-gate and then turn right and follow along for about 300m and then go through a large metal gate on the right just before where a bridge has been removed. Drop down onto the tarmac – take care as this is used by quarry traffic. Turn left and follow down to the road junction. Here turn left and through the 30 mph signs into Harper Hill. Go past a junction, with football pitches and High Peak College to the right. Follow the road along, keeping ahead at the next junction for Town Centre on Harper Hill Road. Cycle down here, with valley and green railings on the left, round various bends and awkwardly parked vehicles until finally a junction is approached with the A515, just before this on the right is Buxton Youth Hostel.

If going into town, go to the junction and bear left. Follow up and then down to traffic lights, go straight across here and rise through the marketplace before dropping to traffic lights in the town centre. For the railway station keep ahead to the roundabout and then right on a small inner ring road, the station is on the left.

17. NEW MILLS TO BUXTON

Distance: 20.5 km/12 miles

Route: New Mills – Low Leighton – Beardmore Farm – Brierley Green – Buxworth – Eccles Pike – Over Leigh – White Hall – Buxton

Surface types: Tarmac, hard-core, stone, earth

Suggested start: New Mills (Golf Course area)

Map: White Peak and Dark Peak, 1:25000 or Touring Map and Guide 4, (1 inch to 1 mile).

Notes: This forms a round trip if used with the Buxton to Bollington and Bollington to New Mills routes, it could also be combined with the Bollington to Strines Station route. At Buxton this links with the Matlock to Buxton and Buxton to Hathersage routes.

Refreshment: Hare and Hounds (Leighton), Navigation Inn (Buxworth), various in Buxton

The Route

This route goes from above New Mills (a former mill town), at the golf course, to the highest market town in England – Buxton. It visits Eccles Pike which belongs to the National Trust and consists of 6 acres of land, 370m (1213ft) above sea level, which was given in 1937 to commemorate the coronation of George VI. It also follows part of the line of an old Roman road from Manchester to Littlechester.

At Buxworth (called Bugsworth until 1929) can be found several relics of the earliest part of the Industrial Revolution. Among these is the terminal basin of Benjamin Outram's Peak Forest Canal (1800) and sections of his tramway. Here limestone was unloaded from the Peak Forest Tramway into narrow boats. The basin is gradually being restored.

The Journey

Section a-b

Cross into Apple Tree Road and begin the descent into the environs of New Mills. There are good views of Kinder Scout ahead on a clear day, with Kinder Downfall being right in the nick. Be careful dropping down here, as the road is very steep in places and you may find walkers with or without golf trolleys. Drop down past a minor crossroads, just after which on the left is a gritstone trough with water feed. Down to the 30 mph signs, be careful here but go straight across into Watford Lane and continue the descent. Drop down and round the bend just before the pylon and to a road junction. Here turn right towards New Mills (Bridge Street); after about 120m turn left into Watford Bridge Road with low bridge notice. Under the railway bridge (Sett Valley Trail but no access here), swing left and then up to the road junction with telephone box on the left.

The Start!

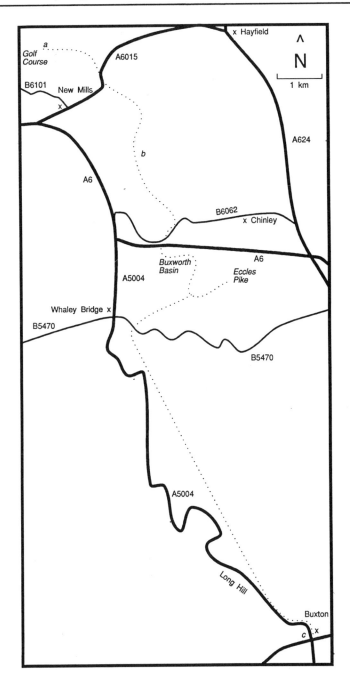

Turn right here into High Hill Road, cycle along past the shops. Continue until just after a church on the right a main road is met – A6015, Hayfield to New Mills. Here bear right into Low Leighton. Continue along here for just over 200m and then turn left immediately after a garage (opposite the Hare and Hounds) into Laneside Road. Climb up gradually between the houses, finally leaving via the speed de-restriction signs, passing a bridleway notice on the left. The road becomes steeper (a hard pull on a hot day!). At a hay barn on the left, turn right into the track opposite (with bridle route sign) and be thankful for almost level ground. Follow along here, bearing left onto a dirt track as the main road swings into the farm yard. Continue the gentle drop here, passing two footpath signs, eventually passing a house on the right and exiting onto the drive. Keep straight ahead, over the cattle grid, over a bridge, under a set of power lines, joining a track from Beardwood Farm, over another cattle grid and onto the tarmac road – called Dolly Lane.

Section b-c

Go straight ahead on Dolly Lane (do not turn right), pass under the power lines and continue for some 2.2 km. Go round to the left and up past Green Head. At Ancoats continue on the present road, finally dropping to Brierly Green and the B6062. Here turn right, under the double railway bridges, past a schools notice and then turn left onto a minor road with 7.5T prohibition order. Pass the Navigation Inn, over the very narrow bridge at Buxworth Basin (have a rest).

Continue up and over the Chapel By-pass and then left into Western Lane. Follow through the houses and the hazards of the parked cars with football pitch on the left. At the end of the houses, bear to the right and continue on the tarmac up a narrow cutting. At the road junction, go right onto the road with an Unsuitable for Lorries notice. There is now quite a drag uphill on this narrow road, stop and take a breath and look at the panoramic views behind. The road then drops to a T-junction with house opposite called Sycamores. Turn left and continue uphill for about 750m, with Combs Reservoir down on the right. At the brow of the hill there is a National Trust site on the left called Eccles Pike. Leave the bikes at roadside and use the footpath up to the top – what views! Was it worth the drag?

Return to the bikes and retrace the route down to Sycamores and then keep ahead, dropping past Ollerenshaw Hall and at Horwich Farm swinging sharply left. Keep dropping on this road, eventually going left over a railway bridge and meeting the main road (the main A6 before the Chapel By-pass was built). Here turn right and then immediately left into Elnor Lane and continue up and through the houses. Where the road forks bear left – note the small monument in the apex of the fork. Continue the climb past Elnor Lane Farm, noting the TV mast on Ladder Hill on the left. Follow the tarmac road, past Wythen Lache on the left, dropping down and then up past Wainstones and finally to a road junction.

Take the road that goes straight on with No Through Road sign. Continue along here, swinging to the left in front of a wall with Rescue Post notice (the grounds of White Hall Outdoor Pursuit Centre). Continue the steady climb – away to the right are good views into the Goyt Valley. The route being followed is that of an old Roman road, the replacement road being lower down on the right. Go through the gate with *Please Close* notice.

Rise past a Scots Pine plantation on the right and continue to the brow. The tarmac surface now ends and the track becomes rough in places. Below is the town of Buxton – downhill all the way! Drop down to the next gate (with Please Close notice) and then in another 40m tarmac is again reached, by a small reservoir and then a cottage. Ahead are Solomon's Temple on the skyline and the ravages of the quarrying industry. Drop down to the main road – A5004 and known as Long Hill. Bear left but be careful, and drop. After 200m on the right is a camp-site and camping barn. Continue dropping into the fleshpots of Buxton. At the roundabout go across and uphill and there on the left is the railway station with original facade.

18. REDMIRES TO HOLMBRIDGE

Distance: 40 km/25 miles

Route: Redmires – Rivelin Dams – Dungworth – Ewden Village – Upper Midhope – Hazlehead – Townhead – Harden – Ramsden Reservoir (Holmbridge)

Surface types: Tarmac, hard-core, earth

Suggested start: Redmires car park

Map: OS Touring Map and Guide 4, Peak District (1 inch to 1 mile), Dark Peak 1:25000 (part of route).

Notes: This could be linked with part of the Rowsley to Edale route and extended with part of the Holme Moss route. It is also possible to mix with the Langsett and Stocksbridge routes.

Refreshment: The Cabin (A57), Castle Inn (Bolsterstone), Flouch Inn and various in Holmbridge at the end.

The Route

The route closely follows the Peak District National Park boundary from Redmires all the way to Holmbridge. It passes several reservoirs, all of which form water gathering for Sheffield and the surrounds. The route finishes in 'Summer Wine' country which is the basis of the Holme Moss route.

It is quite a tiring route with much up and down and plenty of road work, so allow plenty of time. The route provides a varied selection of scenery.

The Journey

Section a-b

Go out of the back of the car park near the notice board and cycle down the hard-core track. The track drops gradually with a very attractive valley on the right with a stream in the bottom (Wyoming Brook). Continue round the bends until a junction of tracks is reached. Continue straight ahead, labelled Manchester Road and Moscar by the old signpost on the left. The track drops steadily, swinging round right over the bridge of Reddicar Clough. As the next section is traversed there are views to the left down Redmires Reservoirs. Continue round the rock outcrop on the left and then over the bridge of Rivelin Brook before rising up to the A57, opposite a small wooden refreshment hut called The Cabin.

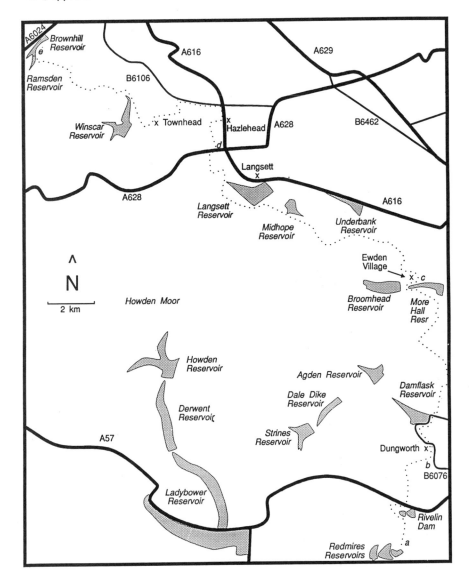

TAKING GREAT CARE, turn right onto the main road and drop down for about 700m round the bends. There is then a cluster of buildings with wooden shed at the roadside just after a Bus Turning Circle. Bear left and uphill just after the shed and behind the cottages, this is known as Onksley Lane. (If you go past the Norfolk Arms you have gone too far!) Rise here and continue round the bends, it's quite a pull. The gradient eventually eases and Ronksley Hall Farm is approached; just before the farm bear right, leaving the tarmac, and onto a hard-core lane that slips round to the right of the house. At the junction continue straight ahead and rising. At the next junction go left and then right again in about 70m. Continue along until a tarmac road junction is reached. Go across here into Beeton Green, signposted to Load Brook.

Drop down this road into Load Brook, a collection of a few houses, then swing up right into Game Lane. Cycle along here, passing Cow Gap Farm Conservation Area, and eventually to a road junction. Bear left at the junction into Sykehouse Lane and head for Dungworth. The road drops gradually, through a road junction and into the outskirts of Dungworth.

Section b-c

Pass a telephone box and follow the road (Briershouse Lane) down. Soon the road swings right and drops steeply round the bends and to a junction opposite Damflask Reservoir. Turn right here, as for Sheffield. Follow round the reservoir and then across the dam and to a road junction, turn right as for Sheffield on the B6077. Rise for a short distance almost to the brow and then double back on the left by the Peak District National Park sign.

This narrow road rises very steeply, at the road junction with seat and litter bin, bear left and continue the struggle. At the next crossroads, continue ahead as for High Bradfield and Ewden Village. Take time as the struggle continues to look back at the views to the rear. Bear to the right at a farm entrance, rising past a house on the left until the next junction is reached. Here turn left as for High Bradfield and Ewden Village. Continue now to another junction opposite a seat and a high wall around a convent, here turn right. After about 100m fork left (with an old milestone with benchmark in the apex) for Oughtibridge and Wharncliffe Side.

In another 200m or so turn left for Ewden Village and Bolsterstone. The road now goes along, round an S-bend and then on to a more level bleak section. Cycle along here – how many radio masts can you spot? A crossroads is reached where there is an old milestone, continue in the direction of Bolstertone. At the next junction, where there is a cottage covered in ivy, go right as for Stocksbridge. At the next meeting of the ways keep ahead as for Stocksbridge, passing a pond on the right. Go over the summit – there is now a choice of routes!

For the adventurous: just opposite Skye Hall Cottage, go left and down the narrow road until just before a gateway with white gate. Turn right here where there is a holly bush with partly obscured Public Bridleway sign also stating No Vehicles Except for Access. Who would want to take a vehicle down here, it would be an assault course for a tank! Go down this lane, well disguised by holly bushes – mind your eyes -and the ground can be very muddy and wet at times. Eventually, the track widens near a farm gate and the surface improves dramatically, continue down, bearing right at the bottom and exiting onto a tarmac road near another Bridleway sign, turn left. The variant described below has now been joined.

For the not so adventurous: continue down past Skye Hall Cottage and down to a road junction, here turn left for Ewden Village, the above variation soon comes in on the left at a Bridleway sign.

Both routes, now joined, continue along this road that is narrow at times and undulates along the hillside, with More Hall Reservoir below. At a junction drop down ahead onto a very steep narrow road and signposted to Ewden Village, Bolsterstone and Stocksbridge. As the road drops, note the gritstone trough on the right as it enters a tree-lined section. Go over the bridge at the bottom, past the house on the right before the road begins to widen and is at reservoir level. Swing round with the earth dam of Broomhead Reservoir on the left.

Section c-d

Rise slightly, passing the private road to Ewden Village, keep ahead and then swing sharply left and continue the struggle uphill. Soon a junction is reached, turn right for Bolsterstone. Climb up through the 30 mph signs, pass a church on the left and then The Castle Inn to the road junction. Go left here onto Stone Moor Road (signposted to Midhopestones and Stocksbridge). The village is now left on a downhill gradient, passing rugby pitches on the left. Go through another brief section of 30 mph near some modern houses and at the next junction continue straight ahead. Another junction is then reached, bear left as for Strines and Derwent Valley. The road now rises into heather-clad fields, then drops down under power lines before swinging right and reaching another junction; go right here.

The road now begins to drop and just before some trees go left, signed for Upper Midhope and Langsett. Follow along with a conifer plantation on the right, ahead is the mast of Holme Moss TV Station with its flashing strobes. The road drops down and over a feeder stream for Midhope Reservoir which is just down on our right.

The road now swings left before reaching a hairpin. On the apex of the hairpin go ahead onto the concrete road (called the Tank Road as there used to be a military training area nearby) with Privilege Footpath sign. Cycle down here to the gate at the end with Public Bridleway sign and go through onto the hard-core track in the trees and known as Thickwoods Lane. Drop down past an arm of Langsett Reservoir on the right and to another bridle gate. Go through and follow along the stream, swinging right over the bridge and then rising with a woodland on the right and open moorland on the left.

Follow the track round the S-bend (as the woodland veers away) and cycle to the gap in the wall with Boundary of Open Country sign. Go through the wall, past the remains of the dwellings at North America (and grassy patch) and follow the track as it rises, marginally left up onto the open moor with heather and bracken. Pass through a broken wall-line and then either over the slab bridge or ford at Ratten Gutter before rising again (with some rutting) to a junction with broken wall and a pair of gate posts opposite with bench mark. This is a meeting with the Edale to Langsett route. The height here is 327m (1072ft).

Turn right and follow the track that eventually reaches some trees on the right and a wall comes in from the left. Follow this track down and round, eventually levelling out with a wall on the right. A Boundary of Open Country notice is the reached. Go right and through the bridle gate with attendant sign and cross over the Brook House Bridge (The Porter or Little Don River). The track then rises to the right and then swings left (follow the blue arrows that denote the bridleway. DO NOT take the routes signified by yellow arrows that are footpaths only). Follow the hard-core track through the trees, after almost 300m a junction is reached with signposts.

The footpath now to be used is being upgraded to bridle route status. There might be additional signposting to that which I found. The route is for Flouch Inn and Hazlehead.

At the main junction go left and drop for about 20m, then turn right onto a path alongside some trees. This track then bears right and follows alongside a wall through the trees – there being the odd muddy patch. Go through a gap in a broken wall, past the rides with power lines. Go ahead, through a hollow with stream (Hagg Brook), and then rise again with a right-hand bend through to a gateway (was a stile). Through this and then between a wall and a fence to the tarmac road and signpost. (Note Flouch Inn to the right for the thirsty!). Turn left here onto the (at present) A628 – TAKING GREAT CARE. Follow along for about 400m (past a lay-by and old milepost stating Barnsley 13 miles, Manchester 23 miles).

Section d-e

Take the Public Bridleway on the right past White Cottages and continue on the walled track to the bridle-gate with No Motor Cycles notice. Go through here and follow the wall on the right – try not to fall into the ditch on the left. There is now a long open section, passing an enclosure with low brick built structure and to the power lines. Here, turn right through a gate and then almost immediately left and drop down to the grassy track at the bottom, just a stones throw from the disused railway track of the Woodhead Line. Turn right here, and head straight for the right side of the house, through the yard – mind the clothes line! Continue onto the hard-core open area and across to the rising track – this is the area of the former Hazlehead Station and junction for the mineral line to the works just to the north. When the road (A616) is reached TAKE CARE. Turn left under the bridge and continue for about 600m to a road junction with Hazlehead Activity Centre on the left. Go left here on the B6169 (Bents Road) and signed for Holmfirth.

Cycle along here for about 1.6 km (1 mile). Where there are some trees on the right, go left at the junction for Carlecotes. The village is reached almost straightway and the 30 mph signs are passed.The road eventually drops into Townhead. The road leaves the hamlet and rises to a summit with poor visibility ahead, here turn right for Winscar Reservoir, Holmfirth and Huddersfield. It is quite a pleasant stretch along here, looking down at Winscar Reservoir (with adequate parking) and then ahead to the dam wall of Harden reservoir.

Rise again and then immediately past the houses on the right there is a choice of routes.

For the good navigator. This route goes through Harden Quarries and poses a tricky navigation problem, it is just about possible with a 1:25000 map – I hope I have got it right! Go through two OLD gateposts where there is a post from which some kind ****** has removed the finger. Continue ahead on a faint grass track and to just past where there is a wall below. Turn left onto the track that crosses and follow through to the main quarry track. Follow the track round to the right and go ahead as if heading towards a small quarry face. Swing left round the back of a large mound and then come back onto the main track. Follow straight down through a hollow where it has been back-filled and then through a gap in a small ridge that has a small retaining stone wall on either side. The track now drops and swings right. Just before it goes left again, go ahead onto a heathery track – do not follow the main track. This track now swings left and then back to the right. Just after it straightens out (about 20m) leave the obvious track and swing up to the left on what looks almost like a footpath onto a knob of rough ground. The track is just discernible: follow it along and it shows the semblance of a double rut. This track bears right and heads towards a tree on the near horizon. Bear right where another rough track comes in on the left and cycle round the ruins of a small building on the right. Before bearing left, look at a white windmill in the distance and down through a gully to gateposts at the roadside, where there is another fingerless post. Did you make it without mistake? Turn left.

For those wanting an easy alternative: continue on the road to the crossroads with house and telephone box, turn left here. The above route joins at a fingerless post.

Continue along this road as it winds along with a plantation on the right. The road goes over a summit and then drops down. At the end of the plantation on the right, there is a Public Bridleway sign on the left, take this – known as Ramsden Road. Follow this rough stony track, past Crossley's Plantation on the left. The lane bears right and the views are now down into 'Summer Wine' country. The track then does a sharp left and drops down on a stony surface to a junction in front of a plantation. Turn right and drop down through a gate and follow the track round to the left into the woods.

Continue down the track and to a junction opposite a house. Go right here and cycle along the wide lane for about 400m; the small Ramsden Reservoir car park will be found by the dam wall.

19. RIVELIN ROUND

Distance: 26 km/16.5 miles

Route: Rivelin – Rails – Ronksley Hall Farm – Redmires Reservoirs – Ringinglow – Burbage/Houndkirk Moors – Blacka Dike – Totley – Whirlow Brook – Fulwood – Rivelin

Surface types: Tarmac, hard-core, earth

Suggested start: Rivelin Car Park (SK291872)

Map: Pathfinder Series (1:25000) sheets SK28/38 and SK27/37 or OS Touring Map and Guide Peak District (1 inch to 1 mile).

Notes: Alternative starts could be made from Redmires Car Park, the Picnic Site (at Limb Hill) or Whirlow Brook Car Park. This route links in with the Houndkirk and Stanage and Redmires to Holmbridge routes.

Refreshment: Norfolk Arms (Rivelin Dams), Norfolk Arms (just off route at Ringinglow), Cricket Inn, Hare and Hounds, Devonshire Arms, Hammer and Pincers

The Route

The route provides a round trip, around the western outskirts of Sheffield and on to the moors beyond. It shows how close a large industrial city can be to really pleasant countryside. The inhabitants of Sheffield are very lucky in that respect. The Rivelin and Redmires Reservoirs are two of the many water supplies for the city. From Rails, much of the route closely follows the Peak National Park boundary down to Totley.

The Journey

Section a-b

At the car park exit turn left and up to the STOP sign, go across onto Rails Road and climb. The road swings right, rising past a Public Footpath sign on the left. At the next left turn (over the left shoulder) go into Woodbank Road. Cycle along here, past Bingley Seat on the right and contour gently along the hillside with good views below. Follow round steeply to the right and keep going up until the present road

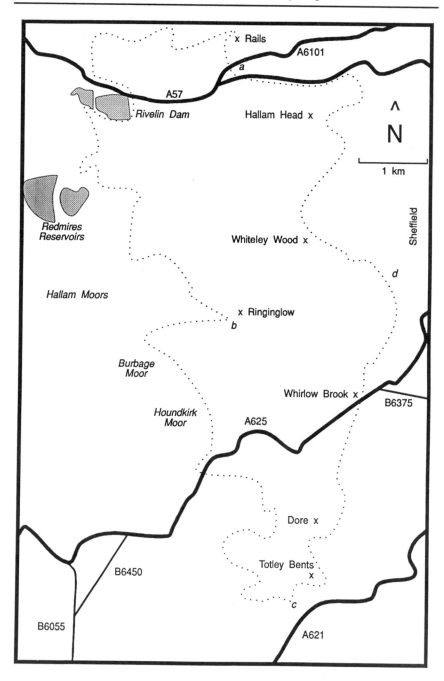

x Rails

A6101

a

A57

Rivelin Dam

Hallam Head x

N

1 km

*Redmires
Reservoirs*

Whiteley Wood x

d

Sheffield

Hallam Moors

x Ringinglow

b

*Burbage
Moor*

Whirlow Brook x

B6375

*Houndkirk
Moor*

A625

Dore x

B6450

Totley Bents
x

c

B6055

A621

levels and swings sharp right. Here, turn left onto a walled hard-core track.

Follow this along the hillside, do a quick left-right near the entrance to Townfield Head Farm and continue on Moorwood Lane until the buildings of Ronksley Hall Farm are approached. Turn left and drop down onto a tarmac track known as Onksley Lane. Follow this down through some gateposts, round some twists and turns until the cottages are reached, brake carefully here to make sure a stop is made at the junction with the A57.

TAKING GREAT CARE, turn left onto the main road and drop down past the Norfolk Arms, round the right-hand bend. Pass the White House residential home on the left and then just before a building on the right-hand side, turn right onto a road that goes across the dam. As the dam is crossed look right and the earthen bank of the next higher dam can be seen. Continue across the dam and swing round right with the road. Cycle along, the road begins to narrow near a small works building and soon becomes a forest track. Follow this as it rises gradually, winding round various bends until another track is reached. Opposite here is an old sign pointing left for Redmires and Lodge Moor, right Manchester Road and Moscar.

Turn left and rise, at times being able to look down on the track you have already come along. Soon the track swings right and runs along the top of a pleasant little valley with Wyoming Brook in the bottom. Eventually it begins to open out and reaches the car park of Redmires and Lodge Moor.

There is now a section of about 5.5 km (3.5 miles) on roads. Turn left out of the car park and rise to a house on the left. Turn right opposite here and cycle round the next sharp bend until there is a farm on the right (Peat Farm) and notice for Brownhills Road. Turn right here and begin to climb almost immediately, round the hairpin and then continue along past Knoll Top Farm and Fulwood Head (with radio mast), there are views away to the left of Sheffield. This is Fulwood Road. Swing round the various bends, passing over Porter Brook before approaching the 40 mph signs at Ringinglow. The junction is soon reached with Ringinglow Road opposite. (For the very thirsty there is the Norfolk Arms some 50m to the left!).

Section b-c

TAKING GREAT CARE, turn right and rise uphill, passing the National Park sign, for some 1.2 km, with Lady Canning Plantation on the left. At the end of the plantation, take the track on the left with Public By-way sign. Go through the gate with a Boundary of Open Country sign and rise gently before the track levels and begins a descent, being a bit rough in places after leaving the plantation. This drops down to another track. Go straight across here onto the semi-walled track with brook on the right. Continue down, with views of Sheffield ahead, to the bridle gate and Boundary of Open Country and Public By-way signs. Go through here and turn right onto Sheephill Road (TAKE CARE!). Follow this road down to the main A625, where a right turn is made. After just over 400m turn left into Whitelow Lane and have a good freewheel downhill for the next 1.4 km. The road has a right hand bend followed shortly by a sharp left-hand bend; just over 100m past this go right into Shorts Lane with Public By-way sign.

Follow the tarmac, which soon becomes hard-core, to a riding school, immediately after this, follow the route signed Public Bridleway to Blacka Moor. Drop down now through the trees, keep straight ahead for Blacka Moor (DO NOT take an obvious track down to the left). Eventually go through a gap in a wall with notice re Blacka Moor Plantation and map of routes – our route is for Moss Road. Continue past here until just before a pair of gateposts, drop down through a ford (with stepping stones) and then begin a slog uphill. Go over the steps and continue along with Blacka Dike down on the right and over a wooden bridge (watch the gap in the railway sleepers). Soon the track veers away from the stream and the grind uphill continues.

The track eventually levels out as an overhead power line is passed, continue until a wall-line is passed through – time for a rest!. Go left here and go downhill, under power lines and then over a bridge, with the track widening. Cycle along until a new set of gates is reached with Blacka Moor Plantation notice board. Go through the gate and then take the track that goes uphill on the right and signed as a Public By-way. Climb up here and finally a tarmac surface is reached where there is another Public By-way notice. Go left here onto Moss Road and drop down, espying a firing range way down below and a vent for Totley Tunnel beneath. Keep dropping until a junction is reached at the bottom.

Section c-d

Turn left opposite Monny Cattery. Cycle along here, bearing right into Penny Lane, passing a pub called the Cricket Inn and rising to a road junction with attendant 30 mph signs. Here turn left, into Old Hay Lane, passing through a wooded area, then over Oldhay Brook and then rising again. The road then swings sharply right and curving left into a built-up area. Keep along here, passing to the left of Dore Parish Church, then the Hare and Hounds, the Methodist Church, Dore and finally the Devonshire Arms on the left before the road junction. Here, taking care, turn right and then immediately left into Rushley Road. Go over the brow and then drop again into Limb Lane. Pass a picnic area on the right (a convenient place for a rest) and then rising into more rural scenery.

Continue along, past some football pitches on the right before finally coming to a major road junction with Hathersage Road (A625). Here, taking great care, turn right and then immediately left through the 30 mph signs for Whirlow. Follow round, past a footpath sign and then to a bridleway sign on the left; take this track. Follow up the initially earthy gully, passing some steps on either side. The track eventually levels off before reaching a metal bridle gate with bridleway notice. Turn right here onto the hard-core track and drop down past the buildings of Whirlow Hall Farm Trust. At the bottom bear left and follow the tarmac surface up and continue ahead with fields on the left. Pass footpath signs at the brow and then drop down, past a school on the left. Follow round the bends and turn left into Bents Drive. Cycle along and then up to the road junction at the top.

Section d-a

TAKING GREAT CARE, turn initially right and then first left (opposite the Hammer and Pincers) into Muskoka Drive. Cycle up and over the summit with views to habitation ahead, and then down to the junction at the bottom with Trap Lane notice opposite. Here turn left in the direction indicated by the Public By-way sign. Pass along by the houses, where the tarmac ceases and there is an Unsuitable for Motors sign, before beginning to drop downhill with paved section on the right. Drop down in this wooded area, over the stream in the bottom and then rising again in front of a barn to reach a tarmac road. Here turn left and cycle along for just under 100m to the next bend, turn right here into Ivy Cottage Lane with No Vehicles Except for Access and Public Bridleway signs. Cycle down here, following the main track to the junction at the bottom. Here, turn right, go over the bridge (Porter Brook) and then climb sharply to a junction. Go straight ahead into Brookhouse Hill and rise through the houses to another junction where there are shops to the left.

Here, TAKING GREAT CARE, turn right and rise uphill for just over 100m and as the main road swings to the right, push your bikes over the pavement into the street that has been blocked off – Chorley Road. Go on this narrow road to the next junction; cross here and continue on Chorley Road. Pass tennis courts on the right, to the next junction. Go straight across, continuing on Chorley Road that then drops to a junction with grit bin and pillar box. Go left here onto Stumperlowe Hall Road and cycle uphill to the next road junction. Bear left and then almost immediately left again into Tom Lane with telephone box. Follow this round to the right and up to the Give Way sign, just past the cream painted house, at the main road. TAKING CARE, turn right onto Redmires Road.

Take the first left into Sandygate Park Road, at the junction that follows almost immediately go right, still keeping on Sandygate Park Road. Follow this down and round through the houses to the road junction at the bottom. Turn left here and follow to the next left-hand bend, here go ahead onto an unmade track with Public By-way sign. Go through the two gateposts and then drop down along the hillside on what is known as Coppice Track. Down below is the busy A57, and over your right-hand shoulder are views of Sheffield. Keep dropping on this rough walled track, past various footpath signs and gateposts until just after it turns sharp right the main A57 is met.

TAKE GREAT CARE HERE. Turn left onto the road for about 30m and then cross over and take a track on the right with Public Bridleway sign. Drop down this walled track, swinging round left just before the River Rivelin, to just before the bridge. Go straight ahead (DO NOT CROSS THE BRIDGE) following the blue arrow. Climb round the left and right bends before meeting the tarmac with a Public Bridleway sign. Turn right, drop down and then left into the car park – journey's end unless there is enough energy for another route!

The Rivelin area from Coppice Road

20. ROWARTH ROUND

Distance: 24 km/15 miles

Route: Rowarth – Lee – Ludworth Intakes – Robin Hood Picking Rods – Plainsteads – Hollingworth Head – Middle Moor – Kinder Reservoir -Kinderlow End – Coldwell Clough – Elle Bank – Hayfield – Phoside Farm -Ollersett – Birch Vale – Wethercotes – Rowarth

Surface types: Tarmac, hard-core, earth

Suggested start: Rowarth Car Park (SK011891)

Map: Dark Peak, 1:25000 and 1 inch Tourist Map

Notes: Two sections of this route go over isolated territory, between Ludworth Intakes and Plainsteads and then from Hollingworth Head via Kinder Reservoir to Coldwell Clough. Serious thoughts should be taken if the weather is inclement, especially wintery. This route links with various routes via Edale at Hayfield and the Chinley Churn route.

Refreshment: Moorfield Arms (near Rowarth), The Grouse Inn (Hollingworth Head), various pubs and cafes in Hayfield, The Grouse (Birch Vale)

The Route

The route goes around Rowarth, over moorland and fell via Kinder Reservoir to Hayfield and then via Ollersett to Birch Vale and a return to Rowarth.

Robin Hood's Picking Rods consist of two stone shafts set into a single stone base, which lies next to an ancient roadway.

The Journey

Section a-b

Turn left out of the car-park and follow the road round the bend and to the road junction, turn right as for New Mills. Follow this road along for about 750m to the next road junction with multiplicity of road signs (and, when I last visited, were in a right jumble!). Go left, exiting from the Peak National Park and then turn right immediately in front of the Moorfield Arms. The road rises to a summit (with Stockport in the distance) and then dropping into a hollow, just before some houses. Here turn right, go backwards and rise on a hard-core track which then goes round a hairpin. The track eventually levels off and then begins to drop, just before the entrance into the house turn right onto a rougher track, go through the stream and then rise again.

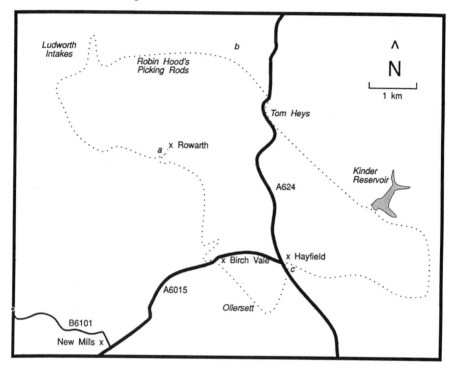

Continue along here, the track levelling on a grassy section just before a footpath sign and the track swings sharply left, past some bushes. Continue and round the next left hander where the rock surface almost forms a pavement and to the tarmac just outside the farm entrance. Here turn right and head uphill, passing Smith Lane Farm and up to the road junction. Turn right here opposite the entrance for Greengate Farm. The road rises to a brow and then drops down under the electricity line. Go past a farm on the right with beautiful wetland area and continue on the road, parallelling the double electricity lines. Take time to admire the views to the rear. The road swings right as the brow is reached. There are views ahead to Bleaklow and Holme Moss TV mast beyond. Drop down and immediately after Mount View Farm Boarding Kennels turn right.

Cycle along here for about 450m to the brow where there is a wide walled track off to the left just before a double bend sign. Take this track and head now for the moorland and skyline ahead. Down on the left are the tall buildings of Hyde. As the gate at the end of the track is approached, go to the right of a small tree on a narrower track and to the green bridle gate. Go through the gate and then follow the track with wall on the right, through boggy patches, passing a footpath sign and to the next broken wall and Robin Hoods Pickling Rods. Continue on the same track to another green bridle gate near Far Slack Farm. We now re-enter the National Park as we cycle along between a fence and a wall, rising steadily.

Robin Hood's Pickling Rods

The track eventually swings left in front of a wall and then to a selection of gates. Here turn right through a green bridle gate and continue on a better surface up to a green coloured post, the remains of footpath signs, at the summit. Now begin to drop down on the same track. Drop down to the tarmac near the remnants of a footpath notice and continue ahead (do not go right). It is pleasant to be back on tarmac for a bit, the speed increases and it's downhill! Go through the gate with sign for Crown Edge Farm, Pony Trekking Centre. Continue on the tarmac, past a tarmac road coming in from the right until a T-junction is reached opposite Plainsteads Farm – and the yapping dogs.

Section b-c

Turn right here, being careful as this can be busy, although it is not a main road. The main A624 is down on the left and you can also see The Grouse Inn. Drop down past the chevrons and to the road junction – we must turn right for Chapel and Hayfield, but the thirsty can go left to the pub and then return! Be more careful on this road, it is busy and there is no alternative – but at least it's downhill. Drop down and then just past Tom Heys Farm take the bridle route on the left with signs for Edale and Castleton.

Go through the gate and along the track for about 50m before veering right and down to a footbridge with memorial plaque for Thomas Boulger. Cross the bridge and then up on the track through heather, passing the National Trust sign for Hollingsworth Clough. Keep rising on the track, a wall joining from the right and then departing again with lone Scots pine. The track then levels off. A TV mast is on the right, our route takes us past there later. Follow down to the next stream and then up on a rough rocky section, with views down the valley on the right towards New Mills and the folly at Lyme Park. The track contours round to a bridge over the bog. To the left is a white hut. Continue to the guide post (1090ft – possibly a bit out) and continue as for Snake Inn and Edale. Shortly you reach a bridleway sign and turn right. Drop down and round above a woodland with Kinder reservoir below. Almost opposite the filter beds below, go through the opening in the wall with deep step where you will have to get off.

Keep dropping down into the trees heading for the reservoir. When a wall is met ahead and a junction, go right away from the reservoir onto the walled track and continue dropping, the track eventually becoming paved with stone. The last section down to the bridle gate is very steep and it may be safer to wheel the bike down. At the tarmac, just outside the entrance to the waterworks, go almost across to a track with wall on the left and rhododendrons on the right. Go over the bridge and then straight uphill on the earth/stone surface between the walls. At the top this reaches a tarmac surface, go straight across to a gate with Hill House Estate sign. Go through the bridle gate and continue uphill on the track with accompanying power lines to the top corner of the wood. Follow along on the more level track to the gateway. Here turn right and follow the occasionally rutted grass track uphill as it follows the fence. After about 250m a throat is formed by the fence on the right and a broken wall on the left. Enter this and then follow the broken wall to the left, running parallel with it. The track eventually becomes more distinct as the wall drops off to the left. Continue on the track to a gateway. Take the track across the field towards the hills, passing a corner in a wall just before another bridle gate.

Pass through the gate and then turn immediately right into a walled track. Go along here, the wall on the left eventually turning away. Keep along the wall on the right, passing beneath Kinderlow End. As the wall on the right turns away head straight to the gate in the fence-line. Go through here and then take the left fork. The next few hundred metres are the trickiest, especially if the tracks are covered in snow. The hills ahead are Mount Famine, South Head and Chinley Churn.

Having taken the left fork follow along for about 300m and then bear right onto a less defined grassy track (the more obvious rising track being a footpath). Continue along, crossing another track at almost right angles and following round left and heading for the upper narrower gate with green post and sign stating Bridle Path to Glossop. Having passed through turn right and head down the track to the next gate. Pass through the gate. On reaching a four-way signpost, continue straight ahead, signed for Hayfield. Continue down to the next gate, having passed through this veer right, passing over a bridge and attaining a tarmac surface. Head towards the houses and going to the right of the trees. Pass the houses at Coldwell Clough (dated 1804).

This is a pleasant drop down here on a tarmac surface, as two gates are approached go to the left-hand one, pass through, cross a bridge and then rise uphill. A bridle route sign is then passed and in another 100m another one. Take this second bridle track across an open field, eventually coming to a bridle gate in a wall. Go through this and then take the lower track which goes straight ahead with the trees on the left (do not go uphill on the walled track). Follow this round to the left and begin the descent for Hayfield. The track has some rough sections on it in places – rocks and tree roots. Pass a house on the left and then a camp site will be seen ahead. Keep following the track down and round to the left again. Just keep going and eventually to a bridle gate near two wooden electricity poles with mounted transformer. Go through the gate (with notice for Stones House Farm), soon being joined by a footpath coming in from the right. Continue alongside the River Kinder, a rough tarmac surface beginning near some houses. Continue along the road, bearing right at a junction, past more houses and then onto a wider tarmac surface.

Follow down to the Give Way sign. Shops and refreshments are to the right; our route leaves Hayfield – go left and uphill on Highgate Road. Continue rising for about 250m until opposite a field on the left a Bridleway sign on the right signifies a route in that direction. Go through the gate with notice Smithfold Farm, going from a grass to a tarmac surface and dropping sharply to the A624 again.

Section c-a

Cross over the A624 (Chapel Road) and to the bridleway opposite with a house (Tan Dyke) on the left. Drop down the lane (tarmac/hard-core), across the stream at the bottom on a track with semblances of gritstone setts. Past the small pond on the left, through the white gate and follow the track as it climbs and curves right into the small valley. As the barn is approached with large white doors, turn to the right. Go through the large gate and approach the garden wall (Phoside Farm). Turn left onto the paving and go to the bridle gate at the back of the barn. Go through the bridle gate (with guide post) and begin the uphill climb for Ollersett.

The track is eventually funnelled between a fence on the left and trees on the right. Follow this up to the next bridle gate. It is worth taking time to look down into the idyllic valley with stream and pool (Foxholes Clough) – especially if you are beginning to feel weary. As open country opens up ahead, follow the wall round to the right and up, past the end of a tree line and with views to Hayfield, Little Hayfield and Kinder Scout on the right. Keep on upwards, heading in the direction of the TV mast but following the wall line. As the wall turns sharply right, another track comes in from the left. Bear right and head downhill to the bridle gate and sign post, pass through and then continue ahead on the tarmac with grass in the centre (do NOT turn right). Drop down on a rough tarmac track, through a gateway and entrance to Little Ridge Farm and eventually past houses on the right. Across the valley ahead are two summits, the right-hand one being Lantern Pike (visited on another route).

On reaching the road at the bottom opposite the Station Road notice, there is The Grouse pub on the left. Be careful this A6015 can be busy at times. Go straight across, bearing left onto the road for Thornsett and Mellor. Drop down here through the 30 mph signs, Magi's Diner and the Sett Valley Trail, over the River Sett at the bottom. After the terraced houses on the right go right onto a rising cobbled surface with bridleway notice just below a white house called White Weaver's Cottage. As the cottage is passed the track becomes walled and rougher and a sign stating that this is a bridleway and not for motorcycles.

Rise here to the bridle gate at the top and motorcycle trap. Down on the right is a small reservoir and the River Sett. The exit here is onto a hairpin on a tarmac track. Bear left and go uphill, and in about 300m another road is encountered opposite some cottages. Turn left here and head uphill, passing a footpath sign on the left and Hext Farm on the right. As the brow is reached with attendant power lines, telephone lines and radio mast, turn right onto a track past a ruined building and former quarry. Cycle along here to Wethercotes and go through a gate. Go straight through, leaving on a walled track beyond.

After about 200m there is a prohibition sign for motorcycles and cars and a dividing of the ways. Keep on the main track (i.e. DO NOT drop to the bridle gate). After about 650m on a steady rise, the track swings right and there is another junction. There are good views hereabouts. Here bear left and drop downhill on a rough stony track, swinging to the left at the bottom. Continue on a varying surface, the small hamlet being ahead and slightly right. Drop down on a stony sunken track, eventually exiting onto tarmac near Laneside Farm. Continue along here to Little Mill, where there is a Post Office, Little Mill Inn and recreation area.

Pass the recreation area, small parking area and house on the right and then immediately turn right into a bridleway which is initially tarmac. Follow this track that soon becomes hard-core. Pass a cottage on the left and continue ahead onto a rougher surface. Rise here to just before a gateway and then dog-leg to the left. Go between a wall and a fence, eventually exiting onto tarmac almost opposite a telephone box. Go left here and follow up past the houses to the road junction, here turn left and in about 150m the car park is found where our journey started from.

21. ROWSLEY TO EDALE

Distance: 41 km/25.5 miles

Route: Rowsley – Edensor – Pilsley – Hassop – Rowland – Housley – Foolow – Great Hucklow – Abney – Bradwell – Hope – Hope Cross – Edale

Surface types: Tarmac, hard-core, earth

Suggested start: Rowsley car park (SK257657)

Map: White Peak and Dark Peak (1:25000) or OS Touring Map and Guide 4, Peak District (1 inch to 1 mile).

Notes: This route could be linked at Hope Cross with the Edale to Langsett route to form quite a long journey. A link can be made above Bradwell to follow the Buxton to Hathersage route either way, there being Youth Hostels at either end. It is also possible, just north of Foolow, to visit Bretton Youth Hostel.

Refreshment: Peacock (Rowsley), Devonshire Arms (Pilsley), Eyre Arms (Hassop – just off route), Lazy Landlord (Foolow), Valley Lodge (Bradwell), Woodroffe Arms Hotel, Old Hall and Cheshire Cheese (Hope), The Ramblers and Nagg's Head (Edale).

The Route

The route goes from lowland limestone areas up onto the high limestone plateau with superb views and quarrying activities and then finishing in gritstone country just below the high plateau of Kinder Scout.

The start at Rowsley is the home of Cauldwell's Flour Mill Museum. The route then visits Chatsworth Park, Chatsworth House being the home of the Duke of Devonshire and is reputed to house one of the country's greatest collections of works of art. After this the village of Pilsley is passed before heading for Hassop and thence Rowland and surrounding areas of former lead mining (now quarrying). The route passes through Cavendish Mill, an area that has been laid to waste by quarrying, and thence to more tranquil scenes through Foolow.

The journey then rises to Abney and onto Shatton Moor before dropping into Bradwell, which is overshadowed by the large cement works, the route skirting this complex. The final part of the route into the Vale of Edale is via Hope and then the old Roman road to Hope Cross. The journey finishes at Edale, the start of the Pennine Way.

The Journey

Section a-b

Go left out of the car park and along to the A6 – be careful! Go across here, passing to the left of The Peacock, the road has a No Through Road notice and there is a post office and general stores on the left. Follow this road as it climbs uphill through the houses and the abutments of a bridge on the former Midland Railway Line to Manchester. Go past the delimit signs and then, at the last house on the left, the tarmac road ceases and the road continues as a lane with hard-core surface passing to the right of the house.

The track now climbs gradually, after about 550m it swings sharply right in front of a conifer plantation and is slightly rutted and wet.in this section. Continue up for 200m to a junction, turn sharp left here on the track that drops down slightly. Keep on and the track will again rise and at the top bears left and into more open terrain. Keep to the wall on the left and enter the walled track that begins to drop downhill. Go down here for 200m and another junction is reached with metal bar gate. Go right here and then virtually straightway go right again through a pair of gateposts onto a rising bridleway just inside a plantation.

Follow up through the mixed deciduous/Scots pine plantation, twisting and turning on the track. Soon a track is reached that crosses, go left. Follow along for a short section before turning off right as shown by the blue arrow. Rise again and soon the track swings left and follows a wall. After just over about 250m go through the gateway in the wall and swing left -follow the blue arrows. Cycle along, first one side of the power lines and then crossing to the other side before reaching a right-hand turn in front of a gate. Follow down with wall on the left to a stile and set of gates.

Go through the interesting arrangement of the pair of gates and then continue across the field ahead in the direction shown by the blue arrow. Go across. the open field towards the woodland in the dip, passing two waymarks and two stone water troughs on the left. Soon a rough track is met. Bear right and follow to the wall and then swing left and follow the wall round to a gate. Go through, take note that the route swings sharp right and follows the wall on the right. Follow until a power line, a gate and a wall are met, here turn left. (An alternative is to go right, observing the notices, and go down on the track through the dwellings to Calton Lees, the car park and then going left through Chatsworth Park).

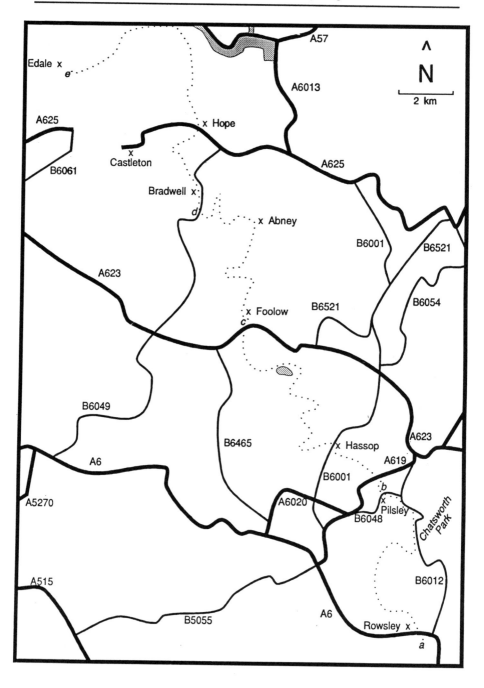

Having turned left, follow the wall on the right until it veers to the right near an electricity pole. Bear marginally left here on the track and go across the field towards a sign post, bearing to the left of the barn. At the finger post go straight across the track, signed for Edensor and Chatsworth. A gate in a wall is soon reached. Go through this and drop down on the walled track through the woodland to the next gate. Go through the gate and have a look at the information board about Chatsworth.

The next set of instructions should be followed closely as no track is obvious. Go straight ahead to a wooden post some 150m distance and then to just before a group of young trees. Turn right onto what seems a levelled grass track. Follow this for about 350m where another wooden post is found. Drop down just past this and then turn left and aiming for another wooden post some 200m away. From here, look left for another wooden post almost 250m away towards the road. Go for this and then in the same line up to the road beyond. During this section, you may well see both sheep and deer grazing together.

Having reached the road turn left (TAKE CARE) and drop down (the church at Edensor being seen ahead), on the right-hand bend you can follow another levelled grass track marked by wooden posts to near the entrance to Edensor. Otherwise follow the road round, both variants then exiting Chatsworth Park over the cattle grid. Cycle uphill, passing the Estate Office and Cavendish Hall on the right, and enter a right-hand curve where warning for a T-junction is found. At the T-junction go left on the B6048, Pilsley and Bakewell. Continue along here until shortly after a left-hand bend and Pilsley, notice there is a turning on the right just after a school sign and signposted to Pilsley Village. Cycle down to the Devonshire Arms.

Section b-c

Turn left here and go on the No Through Road past the houses, after which the tarmac surface becomes hard-core. Go over the brow and drop down to the junction with footpath sign. Turn right and follow down the rutted track at the edge of the plantation. The track soon becomes arched by bushes. The track bears right before making a sharp turn to the left. Continue down the track, now lined by walls, trees and bushes. Cycle down to the gate, through, down over the stream and up to the main road – the A619 and known locally as nine bends.

TAKE GREAT CARE, wait for a lull in the traffic, turn right for about 100m to the gateway with pull-in on the left. Go through the gate with an Unsuitable for Motors sign and continue to the next gate. Go through and press on ahead. There is now a wall on the left and a newly planted conifer area on the right. Soon a more

Winter morning on a track near Pilsley

mature deciduous woodland area is entered and the track bears left above Rymas Brook. This section is badly rutted in places and muddy. Continue along, eventually dropping down right near a stile to the stream. Go through the ford (or little stone bridge on the left) and then rise on a narrow walled track with bushes – watch the eyes! Continue through the gate with wall/fence on the left and hillock on the right to the next gate with views of Hassop Hall ahead. Continue down to the track below and go straight across, round the gate to the left and to a tarmac surface with another Unsuitable for Motors sign.

TAKING GREAT CARE because of limited visibility, turn right onto the B6001 and cycle up to the road junction with green grass triangle. Go left and left here in front of all Saints Catholic Church. (Note: the Eyre Arms is to the right here). Go past the entrance to Hassop Hall and along the walled road, with warning sign about vehicles in the middle of the road. The road soon levels out. Continue along with high wall on the left until it ceases, and just after this turn right for Rowland. Rise up round the bends through the hamlet of Rowland and exit past an Unsuitable for Motor Vehicles sign. Cycle up on the rough tarmac, past a covered reservoir on the left until there is a track off on the left, take this.

Cycle along a walled section to a gateway with footpath sign. Go through this and across the open area to another gate. Continue through, the track occasionally being narrow, and sometimes muddy, through an area with bushes. The track then begins a climb on a rocky surface between walls – be careful of the odd branch across the track and sometimes slippery conditions underwheel! Go up to a metal gate and then turn right onto a wide track. Cycle along here, admiring views to the right but trying to ignore the despoliation on the left. Follow down with a plantation on the right until there is a junction, almost opposite the entrance to Bleaklow.

Turn sharp left here, with wire fence on left, starting to double back to a gate, go through. This track is now followed for about 1.2 km, dropping down through a set of gates until the gates are reached at the bottom. The spoil heaps in the fields hereabouts are the remains of former lead mining activities. Looking straight ahead is a hillside with a building projecting into it. This is a dam wall holding back the water from a small reservoir -all to do with quarrying.

Here, turn right, cross the hard-core road and go through the gate onto an old county road that climbs steeply as it veers right. This is a narrow walled track with bushes, some branches stretching across, and is often used by motorcycles. Eventually the top is reached and views are seen ahead of the Eyam area and beyond. Pass through the large turning area and along the section with man made bank on the left and a dew pond in the field on the right. The surface has now improved and drops down for about 300m to a tarmac road crossing. At this point there is an old barn in the field on the right and the track just traversed has a No Through Road notice.

Turn left onto the narrow road that seems idyllic – but there is a shock awaiting! Cross over the summit and suddenly there is a scene of industrial desolation. Follow down on the rough surface where notices have been erected stating Public Highway. Drop down through the works, taking care of quarry vehicles and it will be seen that this is Laporte Minerals, Cavendish Mill. Rise again on the other side with an earth dam wall on the left. Soon the summit is reached and more pleasant views open out ahead. Freewheel down here to the road junction and then turn right for Stoney Middleton. Cycle along, finally dropping down to a junction with the A623.

TAKE GREAT CARE HERE. Turn right here, as for Chesterfield, go past the Housley sign and then turn left for Foolow. Continue to the next junction and then go left again; soon the 30 mph and village signs are passed and a junction is reached opposite The Lazy Landlord.

Section c-d

Go left and then, in about 100m, take a road on the right where there is St Hugh's Parish Church and a signpost to Bretton. Exit from the village and cycle along with a gradual ascent. The road twists and turns as progress is made towards the hill ahead. The road begins to climb more steeply, and having just passed under a power line turn left onto a rough track. This now contours along the hillside with the power lines running parallel below. This is a walled track, lined at times with brambles; the surface is rutted in places and makes cycling occasionally difficult. The track eventually rises into a section, the bushes forming an archway. Soon a tarmac road is reached. Go left here and then, at the road junction, go right towards Abney.

From here, follow round the bends towards the gliding club on the left. There are good views on the right. Round the sharp bend to the right, past houses on the left and notice proclaiming 'Derbyshire and Lancashire Gliding Club'. Follow the road along in open terrain, past Abney Grange on the right (a detour can be made if you wish). There are good views on this stretch of road. Drop downhill, with trees on either side, round various bends, over a stream and climb uphill into Abney.

Part way through the village is a telephone box on the right. Turn left on to the narrow tarmac track opposite, known as Duper Lane. The track is sunken with banks on either side and fills in during snowy weather – which should make an interesting cycle ride! Gliders can be seen if the weather is right in this area from nearby Great Hucklow. After about 750m the tarmac ceases and the track exits through a gap in a wall into a more open area.

Turn left onto the old county road and go down between the widely spaced walls. The track is a hard-core surface and the views to the right (on a fine day) are of Kinder Scout. The track swings to the right and a footpath comes in on the left. After about another 150m a gate is encountered across the track, pass through and continue on the walled track. The track rises for about 200m before beginning a gentle descent, veering right near a lone tree. The next instructions are crucial as the bridle route to be followed does not begin exactly as shown on the Dark Peak map. Drop down for about another 220m, from where a wall comes in on the left at an angle. Just past this is a metal gate. Go through the gate and head up across the field to the right to a small metal bridle gate on the skyline – this is obvious.

Once through the gate follow with the wall on the right, the track soon swings round a hairpin to the left and follows down a sunken track to a bridle gate. The route continues down Bradwell Edge following a broken wall on the right, meandering down through mainly hawthorn bushes. Eventually the track crosses the wall-line and continues on the other side, now with a wall on the left. Go past the hawthorn bush and squeezer stile on the left and then drop left onto a sunken track. Follow this round as it swings back on itself and drop down to another bridle gate. This exits onto a rough rocky track that soon becomes a poor tarmac surface. Keep on the track, dropping down, and where there is a footpath sign go down left and rise again to a junction. Go across here and then down again, passing a letter box in the wall with VR on it. Drop round to the left and down to the main road – the B6049.

Section d-e

Turn right here and pass the Valley Lodge. Go through the village and then, as the main road swings right, go ahead on the road with notice saying Unsuitable for Quarry Vehicles. Go across at the minor road junction (taking care) and onto the narrow tarmac lane ahead. Follow this along, round the various bends, heading always for the cement works. Go through the green metal posts and continue ahead as indicated for Castleton. At the second set of concrete posts the tarmac track bears left, across an open area, before another set of posts from where the track drops downhill, initially between trees. This confined track now skirts along the edge of the cement works before a gentle rise to some posts – beware of large mechanised vehicles! Here, strictly speaking, the bridle route goes left, uphill, and then bears to the right and back towards the cement works and a bridle route sign, rejoining the previous track.

Having rejoined the other track at the bridle route sign, follow the fence on the right. Pass under one conveyor bridge and then veer right under a second. Follow the fence until the supports for the conveyor bridge are reached, go left in front of them and then right and aim for a lattice metal light tower. Here pick up the bridle route sign for Castleton and continue as the works are left behind. Pass under the power lines and then eventually meet a wall coming in from the right. Cycle along to the green metal posts, go through and continue with wall on the right past the house straight to a bridle gate with concrete posts. Exit onto a tarmac road and turn right.

Drop down this narrow road, past Pindale Farm Outdoor Centre on the right, over a railway bridge and to where the road widens and there is the entrance to Blue Circle Cement Works. Taking greater care, bear left and go along the top level section. Soon there is a $12^{1}/_{2}$% downhill, which swings right past a road junction, heading for Hope. There is a Road Narrows sign; go over the bridge and rise round to the left, passing 30 mph signs. The main road (A625) is reached by the Woodroffe Arms Hotel, with church opposite. Turn right onto the main road with small supermarket, village post office and then just past The Royal Bank of Scotland, and before the Old Hall pub, turn left into Edale Road.

Follow this road through the houses, past the Cheshire Cheese, under a bridge and eventually the de-restriction signs. Not far after this, the road swings sharp right over a very narrow bridge. On the exit from this, go straight ahead onto a track with No Through Road sign. (For those who want to cheat follow the tarmac road straight for Edale). Rise here, over a railway bridge and then swing sharp left in front of Fullwood Stile Farm. Follow this track for another 500m and a gate will be reached just after the tarmac ceases. Go through, under the power lines and up on a very much rougher track. This track eventually undulates as it contours across the hillside before rising to a gate. Go through here and then through to the next gate by an old guide post known as Hope Cross. Continue up to the next gate and four way finger post. Turn left for Edale.

The bridle route now goes through another gate before descending, finally on very rough ground to the waters of Jaggers Clough. Go across, through the bridle-gate and then swing right. Soon this track goes round a hairpin and rises through a stepped area. Go up and bear right over the summit and then drop for some 500-600m to a gate with Boundary of Open Country sign. Go through the gate on the track that leads to another gate near the back of Clough Farm. Through the gate and ford and continue swinging left round the back of the buildings which leads onto a bush lined track that drops down to the Edale road again. Go right onto the road and follow along for the next 2.2 km to Edale – car park, railway station and refreshments!

22. SNAKE TO CROWDEN

Distance: 18 km/11 miles

Route: Snake – Doctor's Gate – Old Glossop – Padfield – Tintwistle – Townhead Farm – Rhodeswood Reservoir – The Hollins – Torside Reservoir – Crowden

Surface types: Rough mountain track, tarmac, hard-core.

Suggested start: Near Snake Summit, Doctor's Gate.

Map: Dark Peak, 1:25000.

Notes: The first section of this route is mountainous and the track very rough. It is really only for the experienced and the first 800m requires good navigation, especially in low visibility. It rises to some 512m (1680ft) above sea level and arctic-like conditions may prevail in winter – you have been warned, use your common sense. In inclement weather it might be wiser to cycle down the main A57 (however unpleasant that may be) into the outskirts of Glossop and turn right at the Commercial Inn, and pick the original route up near The Queen's. The route could be extended, using initially part of the Edale to Langsett route and then cycling up the A57 to Doctor's Gate. It is also possible to back-track a few kilometres from Crowden Hostel and pick up the Longdendale Trail at Torside crossing and use the Woodhead Traverse route.

Refreshment: Snake Inn (prior to route), The Queen's (Old Glossop), Peels Arms (Padfield).

The Route

The route leads from near the top of the Snake Summit (a notorious road in winter) down into the relative shelter of Old Glossop where refreshment can be taken. It then leads through to Padfield and Tintwistle on the A628 cross-Pennine road, where the traffic can be horrendous, especially lorries. The route then uses an old track on the north side of the A628 before crossing and using concessionary routes on North West Water land, alongside a chain of reservoirs. The route re-crosses the main A628 to finish at Crowden where there is a car park, hostel (open to all) and a camp-site. There is a camping barn at the Snake Inn prior to the start of the route and another at Old Glossop (The Tanyard).

For information on the reservoirs and the old railway in Longdendale see the information in the Longdendale Meander and Woodhead Traverse routes respectively.

The Journey

Section a-b

Go through the bridle gate on the rough parking area and past the National Trust sign to Doctor's Gate. Doctor's Gate is a path that follows the course of an old Roman road that was part of a route from Brough (Navio) to Glossop (Melandra). Follow the very narrow track which is almost a footpath, rising gradually. Then drop down to the stream on rough rocky ground and cross – the map calls this a ford! Climb up the other side on a rough track that eventually turns into a moorland grass track.

Cross a small water course on the right and proceed always upwards, passing a bed of reeds on the left. This is an area that requires careful navigation – in snow,

Near the top of Doctor's Gate, looking towards Glossop

the track will not be visible. The track occasionally shows signs of paving with upright kerbs at the edges some 750 to 900mm apart. The track continues in a small depression until it meets the Pennine Way (now with stone 'chatter' surface) and guide post. To the left is the Pennine Way meeting with the A57.

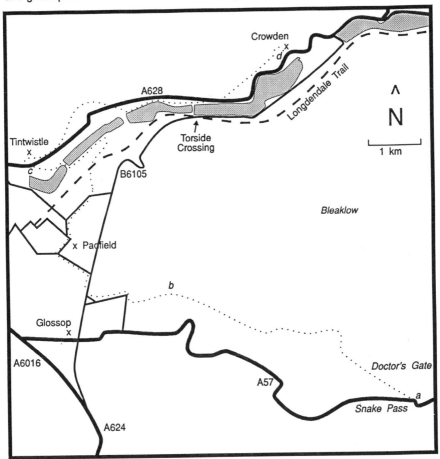

Go straight across the Pennine Way onto a rough track, noting the views in the distance. The track now begins to drop and in so doing is much better defined and should now pose no navigational problems. Follow down, through the rocky zigzags where it is better to push/carry the bike. Follow into Urchin Clough and then along a rough track with steep descent on the right. Continue along, crossing the small Rose Clough and then rounding the bend after which the valley opens up ahead.

Continue down the valley with a stream on the right to the bridge at the bottom. Cross the bridge and then continue to the left alongside Shelf Brook. In places it is good for cycling, in others where the stream bank has been eroded, it may be necessary to carry the bike. Pass through a broken stone wall on an improving track heading towards another stone wall. Just before this wall is reached a green footpath notice is passed on the right. On approaching the wall veer to the left, keeping the walls on the right. Follow along, dropping to another gate and then a meeting of the ways.

Just before the bridge on the main track, turn right and pass over another small stone bridge such that the stream is on the left. The route now passes through several sets of gates, at the second gate look across the stream on the left and to the earthworks of a small reservoir. At the last gate there is a Private notice. Follow down the fenced track, over a small bridge, past Charlesworth Shooting School on the right. You finally arrive on a tarmac surface just before some industrial units.

Section b-c

Having reached the tarmac bus turning circle continue, keeping the industrial units on the right. Keep straight along here to the end where the road name, Shepley Street, is seen and the pub The Queen's on the right-hand corner. Turn right onto Church Street South and continue uphill and into Church Street. Follow this round and uphill again, keeping on the main drag into Church Terrace and on until a T-junction is encountered opposite a cottage called Smith Bar. Turn right here onto the B6105 Woodhead Road, BEWARE OF TRAFFIC as it is somewhat busy. Continue uphill through the 40 mph signs for almost 500m and then turn left into Cemetery Road, signposted Hadfield and Padfield.

Cycle along here for 850m, past Wimberryhill Nurseries, to a road junction. Take the road to the right signposted Padfield and called Redgate. Drop downhill and swing left at the bottom into Padfield. Take the first right (Temple Street), soon passing the Peels Arms and to the T-junction. Turn right and head uphill through the speed de-restriction signs. Cycle 600m to Padfield Water Treatment Works on the right and turn left onto a narrow tarmac track immediately before two small reservoirs. Follow down here with good views of the moors ahead on the opposite side of Longdendale.

Continue across the former railway line (now the Longdendale Trail) until a wooden seat on the left and a track. Have a rest on the seat to admire the views and then take the rough track on the left, dropping down between the trees. Cycle along here, rising up briefly towards Valehouse Farm on the left and then dropping down and following alongside Valehouse Reservoir on the right. As the dam is approached there is a small car park on the left, cross over the dam, noting Bottoms Reservoir on the left. At the end of the dam, follow the tarmac surface as it rises to the left, past the car park for Bottoms Water Park and the North West Water buildings. Go up to the main road, where there is a large North West Water notice. This is Tintwistle.

Section c-d

TAKING GREAT CARE, go straight across the main A628 and follow up Chapel Brow past a small cemetery. At the top, turn right, go past Tintwistle United Reformed Church. Keep always on the higher road (do not go downhill) until the main A628 is again met – the road you have just come along is Old Road. Bear left and, for the next 200m, go along the main road – the worst part of the trip! Immediately before the speed de-restriction signs (the lorries seem to ignore the speed restriction anyway!) and immediately after a house, fork left onto a track. Go up and through the gate where there is a Boundary of Open Country sign.

Continue along this track and keep straight ahead on the poorer walled track (the better track veers right into Townhead Farm). Cycle along the hard-core/broken tarmac track, pass through another gate and then when the tarmac surface appears to go into a field, veer right, keeping on the walled track. Drop down to a bridle gate with Boundary of Open Country notice just beyond, pass through the gate and drop again, keeping to the wall on the right and following a bridle path notice. The path then rises to meet a wider track; bear right and drop down on the wider track to the gate and A628 beyond.

Cross over the A628 (BE CAREFUL), bear to the left and take the walled tarmac drive that drops down. Follow this down to just before the embankment of Rhodeswood Reservoir. Go through the iron gate on the left with notice stating Concessionary Horse Route and Footpath to Crowden. Follow this track along, rising (with the rocks of Tintwistle Knarr Quarry away up on the left) and then dropping down over a bridge and up again to a gateway. Go through the bridle gate and on to the tarmac. Make a small dog-leg to the left and go through the gate with concessionary notice onto the track bed of a small railway line that was used during the construction of the reservoir system.

Go along the track bed for about 200m to the gateway (by the dam on the right) and then follow the signs left up to the gate and into the conifer plantation. Cycle along the track parallel with the reservoir and then to a bridle gate. Go through this, drop down over a small bridge and then go UP left, following the sign for Crowden, to the gateway at the road side. (DO NOT follow the notice for concessionary path). Go across the A628 (BE CAREFUL), to the right, and take the track with a No Through Road notice on the north side of the road. Go through the gate and continue rising along the track. Eventually a conifer plantation starts on the right and the track is fenced. Go through the gateway, past a Pennine Way footpath sign on the left and continue dropping with views of Crowden Hostel ahead. Drop down on the broken tarmac surface, through the gate and across the bridge with the signs for Maximum 3 ton axle load and No track laying vehicles!

After the bridge, continue onto the tarmac surface and with the camp-site on the right. Continue through another gateway and to a junction. Go right for the camp-site; otherwise continue ahead to the next junction with the telephone box on the left, go ahead for the hostel or right for the car park and the A628.

23. STOCKSBRIDGE SURROUND

Distance: 49 km/30.5 miles

Route: Wharncliffe Side – Edge Mount – Wigtwizzle – Midhopestones – Penistone – Oxspring – Thurgoland – Hood Green – Wortley – Howbrook – Grenoside – Oughtibridge – Wharncliffe Side

Surface types: Tarmac, hard-core, earth

Suggested start: Wharncliffe Side (SK296943)

Map: Pathfinder 1:25000, SK29/39 and SE20/30 or OS Touring Map and Guide 4, Peak District (1 inch to 1 mile)

Notes: Quite a lot of this route is on tarmac and hard-core. On a foggy day you don't see many views! This route touches the Redmires to Holmbridge route just before Midhopestones.

Refreshment: Midhopestone Arms, Waggon and Horses (Oxspring), Bridge Inn, Green Dragon and Horse and Jockey (Thurgoland), Eastfield Inn (near Thurgoland), Old Red Lion, Old Harrow Inn and Angel (Grenoside), The Pheasant, Cock Inn and Hare and Hounds (Oughtibridge)

The Route

The route lies to the NW of Sheffield, around Stocksbridge. It crosses some pleasant countryside, including some of the reservoirs that feed this area with water. Again, it shows that superb countryside is on the doorstep for many.

The Journey

Section a-b

Turn left out of the main car park entrance and rise uphill past the houses on Storth Lane, through the 30 mph signs and to the junction. Go straight ahead and rise with wall on the left, houses on the right. Pass a junction and then, just before a telephone box, turn right. Follow this road, round the sharp right-hand bend and then up between the walls to a road junction, here turn right as for Bradfield. Cycle up here for some 1.6km, passing under power lines, to a road junction; go right here for Bolsterstone as shown on the large stone guide post.

Continue straight on at the next crossroads with ivy covered cottage. At the next junction keep on the present road passing another stone sign as for Bolsterstone. Drop down past the chevrons, eventually following a shallow valley on the right to the next crossroads. Go left here, with stone guideposts, for Wigtwizzle. This road now drops before rising after a hollow to the next road junction. Go straight over, keeping Loadfield Quarries to the left. Another junction is soon reached where the route is ahead as for Midhopestones and Strines. About 50m after this last junction, a conifer plantation starts on the right. Take the track that bears off left here with a Bridleway sign partly obscured by a hawthorn bush.

Cycle along the tarmac surface, under power lines, round the bends and eventually an electricity pole with 10 mph sign. Go straight through the gateway, heading towards the houses and into the yard, then bear left and take the track that goes past the side of the house towards a pole with a transformer on it. Follow the track

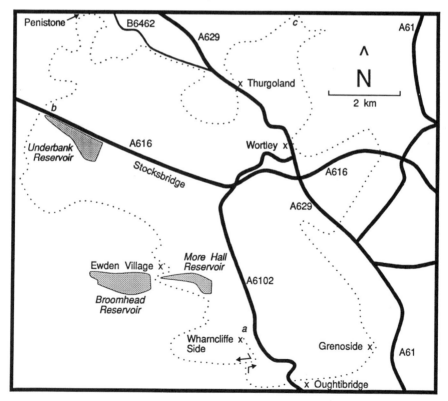

up and round, at a junction with grass triangle go almost ahead, such that a wall is followed on the left to a gate. Go through the gate and onto a walled track that rises, go over the brow and then drop down swinging left to another gateway. The track now swings right into a field. Follow the wall on the right up to a metal gate at the road-side. Go right here for Midhopestones and Penistone, with wall on the right and heather-clad moorland on the left.

There is now a fair tarmac stretch. Keep on this road, passing a road junction and then dropping down round the bends with 20% gradient, over Ewden Beck before a long climb uphill. The summit is eventually attained – admire the views if the weather is clear! Drop down past the next road junction and continue to the next junction. Keep on the same road here, swinging right, down past a woodland into a hollow and then rising again to the next summit, here turn left onto a track with a Public Bridleway sign. Go straight ahead for about 30m towards a field entrance, turn right immediately in front onto a narrow walled track. (For those who wish to miss this continue on the tarmac down to the main road).

Follow this pleasant little walled lane as it swings left at a holly bush, straightens out and passes gateposts and then a pile of gritstone slabs. It soon turns right and drops down between the bushes to a tarmac road. Turn right here, passing the Church of St James, Midhopestones and to another road junction with school buildings on the right and notice for The Midhope Centre. Turn left here for Stocksbridge and Penistone and drop down past the Midhopestone Arms and to the junction with the A616.

Section b-c

It may take a while to get a clear slot here, TAKE GREAT CARE. Go across and under the railway bridge for Penistone. Keep rising and rising, under the major power lines until finally a junction is reached as the road levels out. At this junction go left onto Mossley Road. Cycle along here for some 850m, past a small covered reservoir and house on the right until just before a woodland on the left, turn right onto a walled road with a rough tarmac surface. The road soon starts to drop until another road is reached, go right here and follow through until another junction is met on the outskirts of habitation. Turn left here through the 30 mph signs onto Mortimer Road.

Drop down here, past Cubley Hall on the right, towards Penistone. The road drops into a hollow and then begins to rise and a road comes in on the left from Langsett. Turn right here onto a narrow road with houses. A junction is shortly reached, where you turn left and rise to a junction. Turn right. Cycle along here, the road curving to the right. At the telephone box, turn right into Castle Lane. Rise up and as the road passes a farm building abutting the road on the left, turn right onto a Public Bridleway immediately in front of a bungalow.

Follow this track, past some wooden garages, at the junction bear left and follow the tarmac surface. At the houses the track gains a centre grassed section. Follow this until another junction is reached, go left, pass under the power lines and go up to the junction with a tarmac road, next to a farm and Public Bridleway sign. Turn left here and cycle along to the next road junction after a long straight stretch. Here turn right. At the next junction, keep ahead and, as it swings left, with Tanyard Farm on the right, take the Public Bridleway which goes off left past a seat and towards the pylon.

Follow this walled lane under the singing power lines (when its damp anyway) and when the main track swings right into dwellings, go ahead onto a grassed and walled track. Follow this through to the gate and continue ahead. At the next gate bear left onto the tarmac and follow through to the next gate. Go through and continue to the next gate. Here go into the field and follow just a wall on the right. Pass through the next gate, cross a bridge (1/91) on a disused railway line (ripe for conversion to a cycle route?) and drop into the housing estate, at the tarmac go ahead into a road called The Willows and then a road junction. Turn right onto what is the B6462 and called Sheffield Road. This is now followed for the next 2.2 km. Just after a Jet garage, you can make a detour for 200m down to a Picnic Site.

The route passes the Conoco Black Moor Terminal, then crosses the River Don, Road Subsidence notices and rises to some 30 mph signs just before a road junction. Here taking care, turn right onto a narrow tarmac road with notice stating 'Unsuitable for Heavy Goods Vehicles'. Drop down past a house called The Orchard and then to some houses. Here turn sharp left as for Public Bridleway, follow the tarmac road over the disused railway and continue. The route continues swinging round to the right with the River Don on the left. Cycle along, and habitation is now entered, a small car scrap yard on the right before reaching a road junction (the road just used being called Old Mill Lane). Turn left here and go past a sign for Thurgoland and the Bridge Inn. Keep rising, under a railway bridge and eventually to a road junction with traffic lights – the Green Dragon pub on the left.

Go across here, on a slight dog-leg, onto Smithy Hill. This swings round to the left into Roper Lane and then just in front of the Horse and Jockey swings right and rises up on what is called Thurgoland Hall Lane. After various twists and turns, keep ahead at the first junction, then at the next junction near some houses follow the road left as for Hood Green and Barnsley. Now cycle along past Eastfield Inn and then passing from Hollin Moor Lane into Bagger Wood Road. Bagger Wood is now followed on the left before Hood Green is reached.

Section c-a

Immediately before the main junction with a seat in the middle of some grass on the left, go right into Greno View, follow this round left and then take the hedge-lined Public Bridleway that goes off on the right. Follow this up and then into the farm area. The track goes marginally left near the bungalow. About 25m after the bungalow, go left through a bridle-gate in the hedgerow – just opposite a house. Follow the next instructions carefully. Drop slightly right and follow the hedge on the right until it curves away, here go straight across the field to the bridle-gate on the skyline in the hedgerow. Through this gate and across the next field going marginally right towards the woodland – an arrow on the gatepost shows the route. At the end of the woodland go across a tongue of the field and drop onto a track, turning right to metal gates, Public Bridleway sign and a tarmac road.

Turn right onto the road and follow, cycle along past the farm, pass the notice stating Gudgeon Hole Lane and then past the turn for Crane Moor. There is now a rising section with woodland on the right before reaching the next junction. Turn right onto Hermit Hill Lane and follow along, with Wortley Golf Club on the left, rising up with an ornate stone wall on the right. Just before the main road, go left at Beech House (Agricultural Engineers) and then turn right onto tarmac about 20m before a gate with a No Right of Way sign. Drop down to the main road through

Wortley and turn left TAKE GREAT CARE. As the main road swings right at the Church, bear left into Park Avenue.

Go to the white gates to the right of the entrance to Wortley Hall and onto the Public Bridleway. This is initially tarmac to the second set of white gates near The Lodge. Go through here and continue on hard-core with a fence on the left. The fence then ceases and the track leads to another set of gates. Go through and cycle along the edge of a field, over the brow to another set of gates. After this the track passes a house on the right, joins another track, continuing ahead to some more white gates near a lodge and then to tarmac. Turn right here onto Westwood Lane. Cycle along here, under the Stocksbridge by-pass that was heard earlier and rise to a junction on Storrs Lane. Keep on the same road onto Bromley Carr Lane, signposted for Howbrook.

The road now drops through a hollow and rises up through 30 mph signs into Howbrook. When the road junction is reached go straight across into Berry Lane (with telephone box and seat on the right). Leave the village, go over the summit, round the twists and turns until eventually the main road is reached (Penistone Road). Go straight across into Bank Lane, rise up, turning right near the entrance to Hazelshaw Farm and continue the steady climb. When the road junction is reached, turn left for Grenoside. Continue along here for the next 4.2 km, contouring along a hillside and then passing between Greno Wood and Wharncliffe Wood. It is very pleasant along here with superb views.

Finally the track bears right and drops down through the 30 mph signs into Main Street, Grenoside. The Old Red Lion and Old Harrow Inn are passed and then, just before the Angel, turn right into Stephen Lane and into Lane Head just before the de-restriction signs. Continue past another width restriction sign and into Oughtibridge Lane, after which the width does decrease. Soon a scenic viewpoint is passed on the left, with a plaque, and the road drops down into habitation with a notice proclaiming Oughtibridge. The road drops down through 40 mph signs, over a railway bridge, past a pub called The Pheasant, then the 30 mph signs and the Cock Inn before meeting a main road and one-way system. I would suggest that you cross the road here and push the bikes up to the next junction.

Go across into Church Street and pass the Hare and Hounds. Just before a telephone box on the left, immediately after a house on the right and just before a sign for Church Street, fork right onto a narrow tarmac road that drops downhill. Follow down with railings and brook on the right and then cycle through the dwellings. Struggle up round the S-bends and 1 in 4 hill, passing Coldwell Farm on the right, until a junction is reached – phew! Turn left and rise again, passing Long Barn and to another junction, turn right for Oughtibridge, the circle is now complete.

It is now a matter of reversing the first part of the outward route: drop down here, round a sharp bend and then through 30 mph signs to a junction, with telephone box, in a built-up area. Turn left here as for Wharncliffe Side. Follow down now for some 200+ metres and then as this road swings sharply right go ahead into Storth Lane, for Glen How Park and parking, the route is complete!

24. TITTESWORTH TO CAT AND FIDDLE

Distance: 19 km/12 miles

Route: Tittesworth Reservoir – Meerbrook – Gun – Swythamley Hall – Gradbach – Three Shire Heads – Dane Bower – Cat and Fiddle

Surface types: Tarmac, hard-core, earth

Suggested start: Tittesworth Reservoir car park or Meerbrook Youth Hostel

Map: White Peak map, 1:25000

Notes: This route links with the Buxton to Bollington route at the Cat and Fiddle. There is a Youth Hostel at Meerbrook and Gradbach.

Refreshment: The Lazy Trout (Meerbrook), Cat and Fiddle

The Route

The route goes from the south of the Peak District National Park, just north of Leek, to the Cat and Fiddle public house (the second highest in England), thus providing links into routes in the northern half of the National Park.

The journey passes through an area that provided the setting for the medieval poem *Sir Gawain and the Green Knight.* The hunting ground of the Green Knight is certainly in the vicinity of the Roaches, Flash and the head-waters of the River Dane. It would appear that Swythamley Hall was the site of the fictitious castle in the poem. The legendary Green Chapel is the curious rock formation now known as Lud's Church, just a short distance off the cycle route. Lud's Church is a rock chasm some 180m long and 15m deep, well-hidden among the trees of Back Forest. The cleft takes its name from the followers of a 15th century reformer called John Wycliffe.

The Journey

Section a-b

Go to the reservoir's car park exit and turn left, shortly passing a notice on the right to a bird hide and then crossing over an arm of the reservoir by means of a bridge.

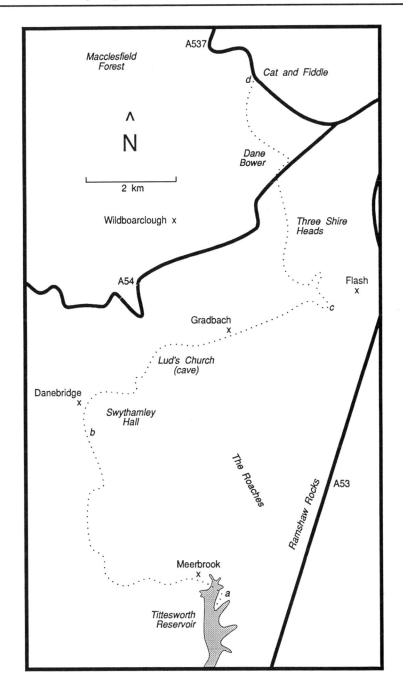

A537

Macclesfield
Forest

Cat and Fiddle

d

^
N

Dane
Bower

2 km

Wildboarclough x

Three Shire
Heads

A54

Flash
x

c

Gradbach
x

Lud's Church
(cave)

Danebridge
x

Swythamley
Hall

b

The Roaches

Ramshaw Rocks

A53

Meerbrook
x

a

Tittesworth
Reservoir

Continue along the road, passing a methodist chapel on the right and into the village of Meerbrook with a pub called The Lazy Trout on the right at a road junction. Keep straight on as for Rushton and Danebridge, passing the Youth Hostel on the right and then the Parish Church of St Matthew. As the village is left the village hall is passed on the right, the road having a slight uphill gradient.

After a right and left-hand turn, the gradient steepens, there being good views to the left of the flatlands of Leek and Tittesworth Reservoir (over your left shoulder). Continue the uphill struggle, moorland with heather soon beginning on the right. As the road swings right the microwave tower on Sutton Common will be seen. The road then begins to drop and, looking left through a gap in the hills to the flat plain of Cheshire, the radio telescope at Jodrell Bank can be seen. The downhill gradient increases before levelling towards a crossroads. Keep ahead as for Wincle and to the road junction with a Give Way sign. Here go right as for Swythamley and Danebridge. The route soon becomes tree-lined – a typical avenue, before a right-hand bend at the entrance to Hawksley Farm and Hollin Hall Farm.

After another 350m the road swings left near the entrance to Gun End Farm. Soon a road junction is reached just after a telephone box and post box on the right. Go left here, signposted Beard Hill and labelled with Coach Prohibition and Poacherwatch signs. Drop down past the post office and then round some S-bends into a wooded area with a stream way down on the left. Drop down into the bottom at Beard Cottage and then climb up steeply round the hairpin of Bearda Hill on a narrow road. The gradient then eases, with the River Dane down below on the left, and a junction is soon reached opposite a lodge. Bear left here.

Section b-c

When the left turn is made, turn right onto a road with No Through Road sign and labelled Paddock Farm and Hangingstone Farm.

Detour: Before making this turn, it is worth continuing on for about 900m into Danebridge where a visit can be made to Danebridge Fisheries (Trout Farm). As the road drops, the sheds of the trout farm are down on the left. Cross the River Dane and then, shortly on the left, is the entrance. After the visit, retrace the steps to the turn indicated.

Returning to the route, cycle towards the iron gates and then turn left onto the tarmac road with signs for Private Road, Hangingstone Farm and Footpath to Gradbach. This is now a concessionary bridle path, so do not be put off by the above notices. Follow up this narrow tarmac road, with rhododendron bushes, over the brow and a house called Snipe, and following round to the right (with the conical Midgley Hill ahead) and soon passing over a cattle grid. The road follows a wall on the right that is the boundary of Swythamley Hall. Follow along, passing Park House and dropping to a junction; keep ahead here and go onto hard-core, still following the wall on the right. Swythamley Hall can occasionally be seen through gaps in the bushes/trees.

Track near Gradbach

This track then swings left and rises gradually under the electricity lines with Hanging Stone prominent on the hillside ahead before another junction. Here, you can leave the bikes and walk up the concession path on the left to Hanging Stone itself. Otherwise follow the concession· bridle-way that has a minor diversion to avoid passing the windows of Paddock Farm. Go across the hard-core area to three small boulders at the bottom of a reddish earth ramp and rise to the gate with signpost (do not use the large field gate on the right). The sign states Concession path and points to Gradbach. Go through the gateway and along the track that parallels the one below going directly to Paddock Farm. Continue between the fences until the track drops down onto a walled track and bear left and rise.

Continue up to a gate with Concession Bridle-way sign. Go through the gate onto the Roaches Estate (owned by the Peak District National Park and managed as a nature reserve for the nation). Go left onto a rocky track (as for Gradbach) and cycle along a sunken track through to another gate with a bridle-way notice. Go through this and then begin a descent. The track now follows a wall on the left through a heather-clad area. At times the track is slightly awkward as it twists among the heather. The wall on the left eventually bears sharply away and a minor junction is reached near an old wooden gate post. Keep ahead here on the sunken track that soon widens a bit. The route still keeps a gradual descent, soon coming into trees. The route eventually comes to another signpost near two large rock outcrops.

Here go marginally left, the bridle route being clearly labelled. (Note: ahead it is worth walking through to Lud's Church, a cave, the route is NOT for cycling). The bridle-way continues downhill through the trees, on a surface that is occasionally rocky and crossed by tree roots. Away down on the left is the River Dane. At the next signpost keep on the present track as for Roach End (ignore the invitation for Gradbach!). Keep following the track round to the right and down to Black Brook and the ford. Through the ford (as for Gradbach), to the gate, through it and then onto the walled track which swings sharp left and rises uphill. Go over the brow, next to a Scots pine plantation, through a level section (sometimes) wet and then to another junction.

Here turn left and drop down to the houses (a scout camp) and tarmac. Follow the tarmac as it rises and then drops down with a large pair of stone gateposts on the left – the entrance to Gradbach Mill and Youth Hostel. Keep ahead on the tarmac, dropping all of the way, eventually passing Gradbach car park. Cross over the bridge on the narrow road, passing a farm before rising to a road junction. Here, TAKING CARE, turn right and continue along here, passing a road junction with bridge, and rise for another 250m, before turning left onto an unsignposted narrow road. Pass New Cottage on the right before rising up through cottages on either side of the road at Spring Head, with rocky outcrops up on the right. The road now enters a long right-hand bend before dropping down to the left (passing a bridle-way sign on the right). As the road reaches the hollow after a very sharp left-hander, take a bridle-way on the left to Far Brook Farm, dropping down on a concrete surface.

Section c-d

Go down the concrete track until there is a barn on the left, immediately after this (and in front of the house) go through a gate with bridle route sign. At the farm here it is possible to get ices, teas and cakes.

Follow on the grass surface and keep to the right of the stakes. This eventually goes into a walled section before opening out and leading to another gate. Through this and to a stream and footbridge. Choose the method of crossing that is most appropriate. On the other side continue in the same direction as before and signposted for Drystone Edge. Follow up this deeply grooved track, through a bridle gate near a conifer plantation and follow ahead until a tarmac surface is reached at Hawk's Nest. Go left here.

Follow along the tarmac road, through any gates and pass Turn Edge Farm on the right where the surface turns to hard-core. Just beyond the farm take the right fork, keeping a barn to the left. Follow this walled track along, at the next junction taking the lower track (which goes straight ahead). The surface now becomes much rougher and rocky in places but is sandy in other places. Keep along this pleasant little valley, past a ruin on the right-hand side and to a gateway, with path coming in from the right. Through the gate and now head parallel to the River Dane, admiring the scenery and waterfall and pack horse bridge. This area is called Three Shires Head.

❏ NOTE: Derbyshire, Staffordshire and Cheshire meet at Pannier's Pool Bridge.

Cross the bridge and then left over the main stream, then turn right, signposted a bridleway. Cycle along here, with the River Dane down on the right. The track can now be quite rocky in places so be careful. Keep going for about 450m and a small stream is crossed. Go straight ahead through the gate and then follow the fence round and up to the left on a grassy track. Follow a wall on the left until a fence-line is reached and then bear left and keep going (do not go through the obvious gate here). Follow the wall/fence on the right for about 125m. Then go right through a gate in the elbow of a wall-line and follow the track to another gate. Go through the next gates (where the farmer marshals sheep at times), into a walled section and then to another gate leading onto hard-core track and bridleway sign.

Turn left here and head up and away from the farm. Struggle up towards the main road, observe the beautiful valley below and the River Dane. Looking away over this to the right are the former Reeve-Edge and Danebower Quarries. On reaching the tarmac road (A54) turn right. Go along the main road for some 2 km. From here, the road swings left and a bridle route is taken going off on the left through a gate just after an old quarry, now forming a small pull-in area. This route gradually climbs and can be quite tiresome with the odd boggy patch. Eventually a footpath comes in on the left from Cumberland Brook. Keep on the main track and a gateway is reached. Go through this and views start to open up ahead and shortly the Cat and Fiddle pub is seen. Keep straight towards this and the road and maybe a welcome drink!

25. WHITE LODGE TO COMBS RESERVOIR

Distance: 33 km/20.5 miles

Route: White Lodge – Deep Dale – Taddington – High Dale – Priestcliffe – Millers Dale – Wheston – Barmoor – Dove Holes – Combs – Combs Reservoir

Surface types: Tarmac, hard-core, grass

Suggested start: White Lodge Car Park (SK170706)

Map: White Peak 1:25000

Notes: The surfaces used on this route are not too rough and should suit a family. There are plenty of meeting places with tarmac surfaces should the supporting party wish to meet the cyclists. The route also links with the Buxton to Hathersage route.

Refreshment: Queens Arms (Taddington), Anglers Rest (Millers Dale), Beehive Hotel (Combs).

The Route

The route leads one from the quietness of the White Peak, through tranquil dales, crisscrossing the busy A6 several times, through the ravages of quarrying and on again to Combs Reservoir. It is a long route but not particularly rough. It does follow minor tarmac roads in places and so please beware of vehicles. Some just do not treat the roads with respect, they seem to change character once behind a driving wheel.

The Journey

Section a-b

From White Lodge car park turn right onto the A6 (BEWARE) towards Bakewell for about 320m and then as the main road swings left turn right into a tarmac field approach. Go towards the gate and then just in front turn right and go to the bridle road notice next to the bridle gate (about 15m). Go through the gate and then head for the top right-hand corner of the field where the steep side approaches the wall. Follow the gap between the dale side and the wall and follow round to the left.

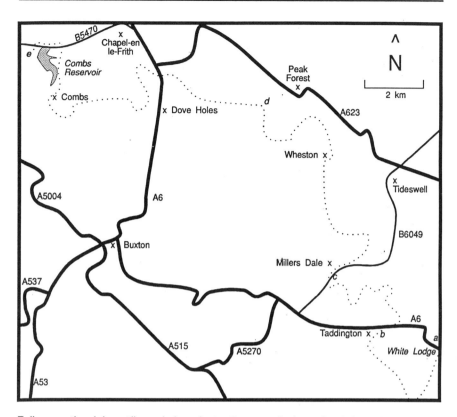

Follow up the dale until an obvious footpath comes in from the right, with stile – the footpath coming directly from White Lodge. Here turn sharp left, DO NOT go ahead following the wall. Go through the small gorge, over the rock step and continue ahead where the dale begins to open up. Just before a hawthorn bush, the path swings sharply right uphill to a junction and conglomeration of footpath signs. Here bear right (as for footpath 2) and following the bridleway direction for Deep Dale.

The route now doubles back on its former direction but at a higher level and is a grassy surface that is just discernible but not obvious with snow cover. The almost level track heads towards a clump of large bushes, then bearing left over a stone slab and rising very quickly to a summit in a shallow depression. Over the summit and then drop down again, bearing to the left of a hawthorn bush into Deep Dale. Bear left as the wall is approached and begin the long shallow ascent up through this Dale. After or during wet weather, the going is soft.

Eventually the dale swings to the left, in the field on the right is a huge section of broken concrete pipe – the mind boggles at how it got here. Shortly after this on the right are the signs of old lead mine workings followed quickly by a dew pond. Looking back over your right shoulder at this point, there is a house perched right up on the horizon. Continue up the dale until a wall is approached barring the way. Immediately before this, go through the bridle gate on the right, (with attendant sign) and continue in the same direction as before. Pass through a wide gateway in a broken wall, past a depression on the right with stinging nettles and to a large metal gate with brothers of the large concrete pipe beyond.

Go through the gate, turn sharp right and rise uphill on the walled track. It is quite a pull up here, but keep up the struggle. As the gradient eases, there is a dew pond in the field on the right. Take time to look around as the views open up and disappear as you progress. You are at about the 332m (1100ft) level of the large limestone plateau that makes up most of the White Peak. Go over the summit and then to Over Wheal Farm and the start of tarmac. Keep rising and about 200m past the farm, just before a summit, turn left onto a walled track with hard-core surface.

Above Deep Dale

Follow this track, known as the Bare Jarnett Road, with its undulations, past a derelict building on the right until eventually, after a summit a tarmac road is reached at High Mere. Here turn right and follow the road round, passing a road junction. Go over another summit and drop to a group of hawthorns on the right. Take the stony track to the right of the bushes. Just before dropping on this track it is worth noting the views ahead, it may be worth detouring for about 100m to get a better view. This is one of the best views in the Peak District.

Drop down this track, through where it narrows and down to the tarmac road in the village of Taddington, by the Bramwell Memorial Institute. However, part way down this track and just before it narrows, there is a gateway on the left into a field that is parish land. It may be worth tarrying a while here and looking at a former village well, known as High Well; you'll find it by going through the gate and uphill to the left at 45 degrees and then into a small enclosure.

To call at the Queen's Arms or the village shop, make a detour to the left.

Section b-c

The route turns right onto the tarmac and then almost immediately veers left, signposted for Ashford and Bakewell. Follow the road, through the de-restriction signs and to the dual carriageway and main A6 at the bottom. Here, take great care, and go straight across to the Low Gear and Hill sign and rise up behind it to a field gate, go through and follow the obvious track uphill. As an opening into a field is approached, bear left into a walled section (not through another opening into a field). After about 10m follow round to the right and continue following a wall on the left, rising, passing a trough on the left and then dropping in a sunken track into High Dale to a junction of walls.

Turn left as the wall ahead is approached, through a gap in the other wall and continue the gentle uphill ride on the valley floor with a wall and fence to the right. Go through the bridle gate and continue until the wall on the right turns a right angle and goes sharply uphill. Bear right and head uphill at 45º into a small dale (DO NOT go ahead following the more obvious main dale). Follow up, through a gap in the broken wall and at the second wall go through the lower gap, keeping straight ahead and passing just to the left of a hawthorn bush. Keep on upward, eventually reaching a bridle gate near the corner of the field and bridleway sign.

Go through the gate and turn left onto the old unsurfaced county road. Drop down and then rise again, passing the grassed spoil heaps of old mine workings on the left and capped mine shafts on the right. Follow left at the bend where there is a nature reserve sign and press on along what is called Bulltor Lane. Over the summit and down to the junction at New Barn, opposite which is an area newly planted by the parish council. At this point turn left and continue down Broadway Lane. Rise eventually past Stopes Cottage on the left until just before the 30 mph signs, here turn sharp right and head down the walled tracked past Lydgate Farm and signposted Millers Dale.

Gradually drop down here and then round the bends into a rutted grass section until eventually a tarmac road is reached. Turn right and drop down to a major road in about 300m. TAKE GREAT CARE HERE. Turn right on the road and drop downhill, round the bend, past a craft centre and then under the dual viaducts at Millers Dale.

Section c-d

About 200m past the viaducts, and about 50m before the Anglers Rest and telephone box, bear left and rise steeply on a tarmac road with Unsuitable for Motors sign. There is now quite a steep pull so take it easy, the lane is called Meadow Lane. The lane starts to level out near the entrance to Monks Dale Farm, various footpath signs are passed. As the summit is approached there are bushes on the left and views begin to open up ahead. Go over the summit and then, just prior to the tarmac roads splitting, take the hard-core track on the left near a solitary tree – this is called Monksdale Lane. Follow along here, round the bends and gradually pulling uphill. Stop occasionally and admire the views to left and right.

Eventually there is a sharp left-hand bend and a junction is reached. Go right here onto a better surface and follow this for the next 800m, gradually losing height until a tarmac road is reached opposite Monksdale House.

Go straight across here onto the narrow tarmac road that is followed for the next 600m until the road swings sharply right. Here take the walled track that goes off straight ahead, the first section of which can be a bit wet and muddy at times. The track gradually rises until the brow is reached, thence drop towards the house and follow the track round to the left, dropping to a tarmac road. Here turn left for about 50m and then turn right, signposted Peak Forest. Follow this tarmac road now, swinging left, for about 1.6 km, admiring the views if it is not misty! At this point take the walled hard-core track, dropping down on the left (signposted Limestone Way) past a small black barn. Drop down to the bottom, veering left into the junction of Hay Dale and Dam Dale, not the rock face on the left. Once in the bottom follow the track that soon rises to the right and follow this until the tarmac road is reached. Turn right and cycle along, past Lower Kempshill Farm and to a road junction.

Section d-e

There is a choice here. Route 1 (tarmac) goes ahead at the junction (Peak Forest), dropping down for about 200m and then turning left onto a single track walled road with sign for Lodesbarn Farm. Cycle up here. Route 2 (with a bit of rougher stuff) goes left at the road junction (Peak Dale) and uphill for about 250m, then go off to the right onto a walled track with rutted grass surface. Drop down here, eventually meeting a tarmac road along which Route 1 is already on. Turn left and then follow the road up, passing a barn on the left and then onto an undulating section 600m or so. When the tarmac track turns sharply right, go ahead (leaving the National Park temporarily) onto the walled hard-core track and along to the next gate. Go through the gate and follow the wall on the right on a grassy surface. Follow through to the next gate. Here the track veers right along the edge of quarry workings with warning notices. Cycle along here, through another gate before rising to cross a quarry track with warning notices about the movement of large vehicles and stone 'daleks'.

Cross over the track (taking care) and continue on the other side, the surface beginning to improve. Follow along, through another gateway (where the Peak District National Park is re-entered) where the track drifts left and there is more sign of tarmac on the surface. Away to the left is Dove Holes. Continue along, over the summit, the track beginning to drop gradually, keeping ahead as the main drag appears to go left, keeping on the walled track. Go through the next gate before dropping steeply down to the A6 – AND HERE TAKE GREAT CARE.

Cross straight over the A6 on to a narrow tarmac road with 7.5T prohibition notice. Take this road, crossing over the Buxton – Manchester railway line before climbing steeply, passing a house on the right (advertising bed and breakfast, under the power lines and eventually to a road junction. Here turn left, signposted Dove Holes. Go along to the next road junction and go left, heading still for Dove Holes. Rise under the power lines, over the summit and then dropping towards habitation. Away down on the left the busy A6 can be seen. Drop down through the 30 mph signs. Keep a watch out for the next turning! Immediately before some bungalows on the right turn right into Cowlow Lane.

Follow this road up, through the de-restriction signs and begin the undulating route as it meanders along towards Combs. Along this section good views will be seen providing the cloud isn't down! The route is one continuous series of ups and downs, passing some rough heather/gorse land where you can practice your wheelies. At one point a rusty old metal post is past at roadside, in the annulus at the top can be just made out Chapel-en-le-Frith RDC. Eventually the road does a sharp left turn downhill, ahead will be seen Combs Reservoir, our destination. This route drops steeply, eventually dropping down through the 30 mph signs into the village of Combs.

Keep going to the Beehive Hotel and then turn right as for Chapel. Cycle along here, under the Buxton – Manchester railway, alongside part of the reservoir and finally up to a main road with 50 mph signs and which proclaims itself as the B5470 (this used to be the original A6). Here (TAKING CARE) turn left (as for Whaley Bridge) and cycle along for about 600m until just before the Tunstead Milton notice, turn left into the area designated British Waterways Board Combs Reservoirs. Drop down beneath the earth dam and, as the road begins to rise, swing right into the car park j– ourney's end!

26. WOODHEAD TRAVERSE

Distance: 16 km/10 miles

Route: Hadfield (Platt Street) – Longdendale Trail. (Bottoms Reservoir, Valehouse Reservoir, Rhodeswood Reservoir, Torside Reservoir, Woodhead Reservoir) – Woodhead Tunnel – Long Side – Salter's Brook – Windle Edge – Dunford Bridge

Surface types: Tarmac, hard-core, grass.

Suggested start: Start of Longdendale Trail, Hadfield – near railway station, Platt Street.

Map: Dark Peak, 1:25000.

Notes: For rides around the reservoirs see Longdendale Meander. There is a hostel and camp-site at Crowden and the area is surrounded by high moorlands that offer good walking and climbing. Please be aware of the weather as the route goes over high inhospitable country. Where the route is shared by both walkers and cyclists, please take care. Walkers often cannot hear cyclists coming from behind – be courteous – ringing a bell or a pleasant greeting is often appreciated. There are stone walled chicanes at all entrances/exits to the Longdendale Trail.

Refreshment: Various pubs in Padfield/Hadfield, Stanhope Arms (Dunford Bridge)

The Route

This route uses part of the Trans-Pennine Trail for walkers and cyclists (and where possible horse-riders and the disabled) which extends from Liverpool to Hull, it then continues on the continent from Rotterdam to Istanbul. Parts of the trail are still in the making and at the time of writing this book not all parts are open. The Trail will also have links to Manchester, Sheffield, Chesterfield, Leeds and York.

The Longdendale Trail is formed from part of the first railway link between Manchester and Sheffield – the Sheffield, Ashton under Lyne and Manchester Railway. Work was started in 1839 and involved the building of two long single line tunnels (4.82 km or 3 miles, 22 yards). The first bore was opened for traffic six years later in 1845, the second bore being opened in 1852. At this time they were the longest tunnels in the world. The depth of the longest ventilation shaft is some 176m (579ft). These were replaced by a single bore tunnel with twin tracks in 1953, just prior to electrification of the line. The original bores are used for carrying electrical conductors across the Pennines instead of a pylon route overhead and subject to the savagery of the winter weather.

The line took heavy mineral traffic across the Pennines plus passenger trains (it's a pity the line isn't still open to take heavy juggernauts off the parallel road). The passenger service to Sheffield was withdrawn in 1970 and the line between Hadfield and Penistone finally closed in 1981, having given 136 years of use. The electrification was at 1500V DC and the locomotives used were very box-like, one of them was named Tommy. Hadfield now serves as the terminus of the line from Manchester.

The Woodhead Tunnel construction took its toll on the navvies building it who worked in atrocious conditions, at least 32 were killed and 142 injured. During the construction of the second tunnel some 28 navvies died from cholera but the deaths due to injuries were less than those for the first tunnel. Many navvies who died were buried at the small St James' Church on the north side of the valley and can be seen from the Longdendale Trail. (For further information, see *The Railway Navvies* by Terry Coleman or *The Sheffield, Ashton under Lyne and Manchester Railway* by Martin Bairstow).

For information about the water works in the valley, please see the route entitled "Longdendale Meander".

The Journey

Section a-b

Starting from Hadfield (Platt Street), just follow the trail! A fair amount of work has gone into the making of the trail, respect the effort that others have made and keep to the side allocated for cyclists and walkers. Go under the over-bridge and then cross sides as the footpath/cycle and horse route transpose. Follow along initially Bottoms Reservoir where water skiing can occasionally be seen. The trail is on a steadily rising gradient, the locomotive crew must have had some superb views along here. The reservoirs of Valehouse and Rhodeswood are gradually passed with Bramah Edge away up on the right. The site of the old level crossing at Torside is reached and possible attendant smells from the maggot farm nearby – depends on the wind direction!

Go across here, through the chicane, and continue along the trail. After just over 1 km Torside Information Centre is passed, a convenient point for any accompanying

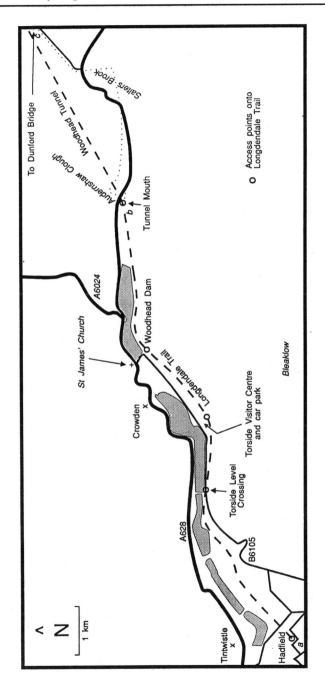

the ride to provide sustenance. It is common to see sailing on Torside Reservoir. As the end of Torside Reservoir is approached, across on the other side is Crowden Hostel (open to all) and the small building of St James' Church – mentioned earlier. After this point the trail rises to cross the B6105 – this rise was not on the original railway line, it has been caused by the raising of the dam across Woodhead Reservoir. It should be noted that power lines are followed all the way up the valley.

Cross the road and pass through the remains of Crowden Station (the old railway cottages are to the right) and continue along the south side of Woodhead Reservoir. "Nine Holes" Bridge (on the A628) is across the water along with the attendant heavy traffic. Eventually the reservoir dwindles to a stream – the River Etherow, the electricity lines disappear underground and the platforms are passed of the old Woodhead station just before the tunnel entrances. The old station houses are on the right.

Woodhead Tunnel

Section b-c

As the new tunnel mouth is approached, bear to the right on a gravel track and rise steeply passing the car parking area. By the top end of the car park, take the grassy track that goes back and up over your left shoulder. On reaching the main road, go through the gate and straight across to another gate on a small car parking area – TAKE GREAT CARE BECAUSE THE TRAFFIC DOESN'T CARE ABOUT YOU! Pass through this and follow the track up, with Audernshaw Clough down on the left. Keep rising until crossing the route of an old road, turn right onto this. On this ascent, the remains of the red bricks are from the dismantled air shaft on one of the old tunnel bores.

Continue along this old hard-core road, rising at first, and then, after a junction with a track coming in from the left, the route begins a slow descent. *Please note:* there is no right of way on the track that goes into the moor, in fact it finishes at Greystone Edge Quarries (now disused). Continue the slow descent until a gate is reached on the A628. Cross over here (TAKING GREAT CARE) and through a gap in the crash barriers and drop downhill with a wall on the right to the old packhorse bridge. It is worth stopping here for a rest and looking at Salter's Brook Bridge on the main road.

Salter's Brook

Continue uphill from the bridge, with a wall on the right and passing the remains of an old inn on the left – called by some The Angel and by others The Crown. The track eventually levels out. Continue until about 50m before a small group of trees and then take the track going off on the left, rising uphill before levelling out. The track passes through a gate in a snow fence and finishes at the road sign on the A628, opposite a road labelled Windle Edge. The road sign has a grid reference on it, 141006, and is at a height of 417m (1367 feet) above sea level.

Go straight across on to Windle Edge that is signposted for Dunford Bridge – BE CAREFUL CROSSING AS IT IS A NASTY BEND. Follow the minor road as it rises and bears to the right, noting the views across moorland to the south. The road eventually begins to drop passing a car park with picnic tables by Winscar reservoir and then into Dunford Bridge and the Stanhope Arms.

NOTE: It is possible to travel further on the old railway line from Dunford Bridge towards Penistone. At present, it is not an official route, but it will lead you near to Ecklands where there is a bridge missing. The section may soon be opened but, at the time of writing, it still belongs to British Rail.

Additional Suggestions

This section contains a few suggestions on connecting routes to make longer journeys. There are many combinations and these represent only a small selection. There are also other by-ways in existence and these could be used. Many additional variations can also be made by use of my first book *Off-Beat Cycling and Mountain Biking in the Peak District* (Sigma Press). However, DO NOT CYCLE ON FOOTPATHS.

Buxton Big Circuit (approximately 130 km/81 miles)

Use the Buxton to Bollington route and then follow through on the Bollington to New Mills route as far as Bottoms Hall. Here use the Marple to Chinley route to Birch Vale. From this point cycle down the Sett Valley Trail and then reverse part of the Low Bradfield to Hayfield route through to Hope Cross (which goes via Edale). From Hope Cross use the Edale to Langsett route through to Langsett. From Langsett pick up and reverse part of the Redmires to Holmbridge route through to Redmires. From Redmires, use the Houndkirk and Stanage route to Hathersage from where the Buxton to Hathersage route can be reversed back to the starting point.

Edale to Marsden (approximately 55 km/34 miles)

Take the Edale to Langsett route through to Langsett, then pick up the Redmires to Holmbridge route to Ramsden Reservoir. From here use the Holme Moss route to Meltham. From here use the B6107 for 6km (3.8 miles) to Marsden. *Note:* It is hoped that in the near future a longer but more interesting route via Wessenden Head will be available.

Langsett to Dovestones (approximately 52 km/33 miles)

Use the Langsett Round route to Townhead and then pick up the Redmires to Holmbridge route to near Ramsden Reservoir. From here use the Holme Moss route via Digley Dam to Meltham. From Meltham make a connection to Marsden using the B6107. Pick up the Marsden route and cycle through to Diggle and then use the Dovestones Round route as far as Dovestones Reservoir.

Matlock to Marple (approximately 63 km/39 miles)

Use the Matlock to Buxton route to Buxton, then pick up and reverse the New Mills to Buxton route. At New Mills golf course connect with and reverse the New Mills to Bollington route as far as Marple.

Meerbrook to Langsett (approximately 69 km/43 miles)

This route links the Youth Hostels at Meerbrook, Gradbach, Buxton, Edale and Langsett. Use the Tittesworth to Cat and Fiddle route to the Cat and Fiddle, then reverse a small section of the Buxton to Bollington route into Buxton. From Buxton use the Buxton to Hathersage route to Bradwell and then pick up the latter part of the Rowsley to Edale route. The Edale to Langsett route can then be picked up at Hope Cross or at Edale.

Rowsley to Padfield (approximately 82 km/51 miles)

The cycle ride takes a somewhat roundabout route. Use the Rowsley to Edale route to Bradwell and then pick up the Buxton to Hathersage route through to Hathersage. From here, use part of the Houndkirk and Stanage route to Redmires Reservoir, from where the Redmires to Holmbridge route can be used to Langsett. From here use the Langsett Round route to near Windleden reservoir and then pick up the Woodhead Traverse route that takes you through to Padfield.

Appendix

Cycle Hire

The following is a list of cycle hire centres, it is not comprehensive. Intending borrowers should telephone to find out information before turning up to hire. They may not necessarily hire out mountain bikes.

Ashbourne	0335 43156
Bollington	0625 72681
Carsington	0629 85478/85648
Derwent (Fairholmes)	0433 651261
Great Longstone	0629 640507
Hartington	0298 84459
Hathersage	0433 50345
Hayfield	0663 746222
Hayfield (Buckingham's)	061 477 7346/0831 196209
Matlock	0629 582089
Middleton Top	0629 823204
Over Haddon	0629 814195
Parsley Hay	0298 84493
Peak Forest Rough Guide	0298 77059
Priestcliffe (Cycle Safaris)	0298 85757
Thorpe	0335 29410
Tideswell	0298 872118
Tissington	0335 25244
Waterhouses	0538 308609
	0538 308313
Mobile Mountain Bike Hire	0226 288350 (day-time)
(Barnsley)	0226 203896 (evenings)
	0226 791575 (evenings)
Inter Peak Cycling	0332 76044

Cycle Hire

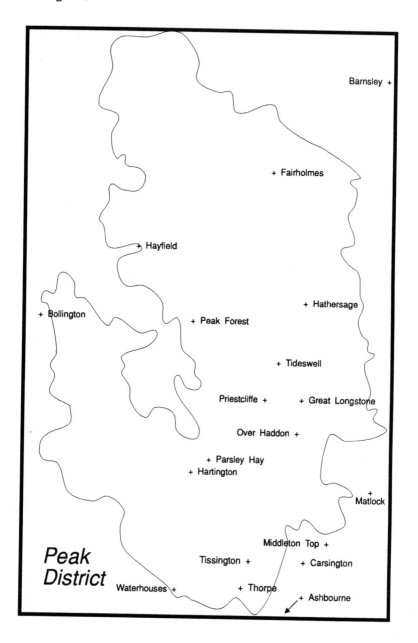

Barnsley +

+ Fairholmes

Hayfield

+ Hathersage

+ Bollington   + Peak Forest

+ Tideswell

Priestcliffe +   + Great Longstone

Over Haddon +

+ Parsley Hay
+ Hartington

+ Matlock

Middleton Top +

Peak
District   Tissington +   + Carsington

Waterhouses +   + Thorpe

+ Ashbourne

YHA Locations

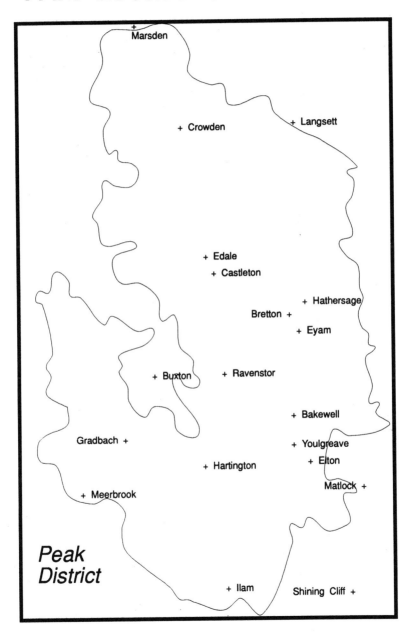

+ Marsden

+ Crowden

+ Langsett

+ Edale

+ Castleton

+ Hathersage

Bretton +

+ Eyam

+ Buxton

+ Ravenstor

+ Bakewell

Gradbach +

+ Youlgreave

+ Elton

+ Hartington

Matlock +

+ Meerbrook

Peak District

+ Ilam

Shining Cliff +

Cycling with Sigma . . .

. . . just the start of our series of cycling books!

Available April 1993:

OFF-BEAT CYCLING & MOUNTAIN BIKING IN THE PEAK DISTRICT
– Clive Smith

MORE OFF-BEAT CYCLING IN THE PEAK DISTRICT
– Clive Smith

50 BEST CYCLE RIDES IN CHESHIRE
– edited by Graham Beech

Available June 1993:

BY-WAY TRAVELS SOUTH OF LONDON
– Geoff Marshall

Available October 1993:

BY-WAYS BIKING IN THE CHILTERNS

– Henry Tindell

Explore the countryside with Sigma!

We have a wide selection of guides to individual towns, plus outdoor activities centred on walking and cycling in the great outdoors throughout England and Wales. This is a recent selection:

PEAK DISTRICT DIARY – Roger Redfern
An evocative book, celebrating the glorious countryside of the Peak District. The book is based on Roger's popular column in *The Guardian* newspaper and is profusely illustrated with stunning photographs. *£6.95*

I REMAIN, YOUR SON JACK – J. C. Morten (edited by Sheila Morten)
A collection of almost 200 letters, as featured on BBC TV, telling the moving story of a young soldier in the First World War. Profusely illustrated with contemporary photographs. *£8.95*

There are many books for outdoor people in our catalogue, including:

RAMBLES IN NORTH WALES
– Roger Redfern

HERITAGE WALKS IN THE PEAK DISTRICT
– Clive Price

EAST CHESHIRE WALKS
– Graham Beech

WEST CHESHIRE WALKS
– Jen Darling

WEST PENNINE WALKS
– Mike Cresswell

NEWARK AND SHERWOOD RAMBLES
– Malcolm McKenzie

RAMBLES AROUND NOTTINGHAM & DERBY
– Keith Taylor

RAMBLES AROUND MANCHESTER
– Mike Cresswell

WESTERN LAKELAND RAMBLES
– Gordon Brown

WELSH WALKS:
Dolgellau and the Cambrian Coast
– Laurence Main and Morag Perrott

WELSH WALKS:
Aberystwyth and District
– Laurence Main and Morag Perrott

– all of these books are currently £6.95 each.

For long-distance walks enthusiasts, we have several books including:

THE GREATER MANCHESTER BOUNDARY WALK
– Graham Phythian

THE THIRLMERE WAY
– Tim Cappelli

THE FURNESS TRAIL
– Tim Cappelli

THE MARCHES WAY
– Les Lumsdon

– all £6.95 each

We also publish:

A guide to the 'Pubs of Old Lancashire'

A fabulous series of 'Pub Walks' books for just about every popular walking area in the UK, all featuring access by public transport

A new series of investigations into the Supernatural, Myth and Magic

Superb illustrated books on Manchester's football teams

– plus many more entertaining and educational books being regularly added to our list.

All of our books are available from your local bookshop. In case of difficulty, or to obtain our complete catalogue, please contact:

Sigma Leisure,

1 South Oak Lane,

Wilmslow, Cheshire SK9 6AR

Phone: 0625 – 531035 Fax: 0625 – 536800

ACCESS and VISA orders welcome – call our friendly sales staff or use our 24 hour Answerphone service! Most orders are despatched on the day we receive your order – you could be enjoying our books in just a couple of days.

Cycling Notes & Diary

Cycling Notes & Diary

Cycling Notes & Diary